Gail Pope & Keith Hammond

Fast Food
Toys

Expanded 2nd Edition
with Updated Values

4880 Lower Valley Road, Atglen, PA 19310 USA

DEDICATION

I would like to dedicate this book to my best friend and husband of 27 years, Frank, who endured all and who is a skilled craftsman, modeler, and collector of toys and trains, and to my sister Mrs. Linda Sue Davis, who started me on this hobby. Special Thanks to Joanne and Keith Hammond who ameliorated my collection.

Library of Congress Cataloging-in-Publication Data

Pope, Gail.
Fast food toys: with values/Gail Pope
& Keith Hammond.
p. cm.--(A Schiffer book for collectors)
ISBN 0-7643-0321-X
1. Toys--Collectors and collecting--United
States--Catalogs.
2. Premiums (Retail trade)--Collectors and collecting--United
States--Catalogs.
3. Fast food restaurants--Collectibles--Catalogs.
I. Hammond, Keith, 1960-
II. Title.
III. Series.
NK9509.P66   1996
688.7'2'0973075--dc20   95-36310
CIP

Revised price guide 1998
Copyright © 1998 by Gail Pope & Keith Hammond

ISBN: 0-7643-0321-X
Printed in China
1 2 3 4

Published by Schiffer Publishing Ltd.
4880 Lower Valley Road
Atglen, PA 19310
E-mail:schifferbk@aol.com

Please write for a free catalog.
This book may be purchased from the publisher.
Please include, $3.95 for shipping.
Try your bookstore first.

CONTENTS

INTRODUCTION

     In the summer of 1990 "everybody" was talking about the first set of Hardee's California Raisin figurines that had just sold for $40.00 at an auction. These things were freebies, given away in the kid's meals. They are cute. The TV advertisements were appealing, the most interesting commercial of the season. And now somebody had paid forty dollars for them.

     We are a generation who have learned that anything that has ever been given away has become collectible and desirable. Toys have been given away in cereal boxes for many years. Promotions for kid's meals seem to have begun in the 1960s with activity bags and boxes and moved on to small rubber figurines, rings, and pencils, etc. These are all collectible, however indistinguishable from the same retail products. Since the mid-eighties, the fast-food chains have had well-painted and designed toys to give away, many in connection with a motion picture, TV cartoon series, or other promotion.

THANKS AND UPDATES

My sincere appreciation to all of the hard working fast food employees! Their jobs are hot and long and they sure have to hustle the whole day. Many thanks for a great job! We collectors thank you for your patience in answering our pleas of "Which toy do you have today?" I try to go at unbusy times, which is not always easy. I hope that all collectors try to be considerate. Many adults and kids are now holding on to more of these collectibles. At most yard sales and flea markets the price is double what it was 2 years ago, and toy dealers are asking book value for a lot of these toys. Some of the newest sets are so popular they demand high prices immediately. It seems that a lot of the toys have increased in physical size from 3 inches to 4 or more inches, which may also change the desirability. My local McDonald's gave away 2 different foreign sets as fill-ins this past year. I can only assume this was done across the country with other sets. Therefore the foreign toy prices are lower which makes it good for people who want to collect these toys also.

I would like to thank the many people who have helped and supported me in my collecting endeavors, among whom are: Frank Duszczak, Linda Sue Davis, Jerry Davis, Maggie Pope, Sabrina Hawkey, Samantha Hawkey, Jarrett Smith, Teresa Hamlin, Randy Hamlin, Keith Hammond, Joanne Hammond, Willie Krichinsky, Ella Krichinsky, Lois Ann Wood, Jerome Harris, Julius Harris, Tyrone Harris, Attlene Harris, Jeremy Wood, Taylor Wood, Karen Wilson, Brandi Van Cleef, Nestor Gil, Reggie Johnson, Mary Morgan, Nathan Morgan, Matthew Morgan, Carl Morgan, Zachery Morgan, Laura Magyar, Courtney Magyar, Phillip Magyar, Angela Carmichael, Lindy Ziegenfuss, Carolyn Mishoe, Stan Duszczak, Donna Duszczak, Greg Hines, Florence Dingle, Sandy George, Carol Kwiatowski, Debrah Strait, Lamont Clark, Charles Jackson, Allison Young, Maryann Stocklingsky, Amy Hynes, Susan Booth, Jackie Booth, Kyle Booth, Edie Goldie, Boo-Boo Howard, Louise Bell, Julian Buonomo, Joyce Losonsky, Jim Bowles, Michelle Bullard, Mandy Walker, Marie Wohlfeld, Jessica Booth, Jason Booth, Kate Uibel, Steve Rausch, Paul David Duszczak Sutton, Linda Gail Duszczak Sutton, Laura Ann Duszczak Sutton, Bob Rupp, Bobby Newbury, Marcus Jones, Brian Maida, Keith Scott, William Buffalo, Buffy Buffalo, Shaun Rice, Bessie Woytalewicz, Stedman Williams, Terrance Williams, Henry Williams, Jim Martin, Paul Nickas, Lois Adkins, Joey Nicholas, Brenda Surber, Pam Carmichael, Keith Houell, Tony Triano, Rick Jones, Henry Brewster, Roy Dowell, Ron Cox, Stacey Yancy.

USING THIS BOOK

EVERY TOY THAT THE RESTAURANTS OFFER IN KID'S MEALS IS HIGHLY COLLECTIBLE. Included in this book are most of the popular figurine and figurine-oriented sets that have been offered as premiums by the "fast food" and other restaurants, allowing freedom for creative expressions for the characters. The vehicles and sports interests are also included. A special section is devoted to plush and pieces which are larger than the standard 3" size. The sets show, in color, which pieces belong to which characters and which characters are in a set.

The sets are listed according to the restaurant which offered the toys in their kid's meals and/or sold them over the counter. Some of the toys were only sold by the restaurants, not used as premiums in the kid's meals. The restaurants are in alphabetical order in this book. Most of the sets are in alphabetical order according to the name of the set, but for practical or photographic reasons this is not always the case, so be sure to look around. The foreign 3" toys are in a separate section. The plush and larger-than-3" toys are in another section. The mold markings that are listed for one piece are not necessarily on all pieces in the set, there are some differences.

When there are "costumes" for the characters, they are usually two pieces that snap together around the character. Robath in the Swan Princess (Hardee's) only has one front body mask instead of the two pieces.

Some items in a set are the same figures in different colors. Only one of a color are shown for most sets with the other variations listed, unless there is a significant difference. Many of the same figurines do have slight or even major color variations due to the various dye lots of the paints used.

The size of most of these toys is about 3 inches tall or long, within an inch. Any significant discrepancy is noted in the comments with each set.

The personal trademarked characters for each restaurant are grouped together in their various sets under the restaurant's name for easy identification.

The contents of this book are the personal property of the authors who are not in any way associated with any restaurant or any reflection thereof. The restaurants are listed only as the source of the toys. This book is concerned only with the toys, not the restaurants which gave them out with kid's meals or otherwise sold them.

PRICES

It seems like the prices from many dealers are slightly down from last year as more people collect and seek out these toys. Another dealer has almost doubled his prices recently. Prices are all over the board. If you need a certain piece to complete a set or list, you might be willing to pay more for it. There are no fixed prices when you deal for collectibles — some dealers do barter. The prices listed here are some average asking prices for the toy in mint condition to MIP that dealers seem to be charging. In general the rarer-found sets, the better quality sets, the most popular characters, and the sets that have to be imported to any area seem to be worth a little more. The Under-3 toys are usually worth a lot more (2 to 5 times as much in some cases) than any in the regular offering. Usually the whole set is worth more money than the sum of the individual pieces.

PVC

There is a whole new generation of toys on the market with the invention of PVC (short for poly-vinyl-chloride, commonly used in plumbing and outdoor furniture and toys). Children's toys that are made with PVC have become practically indestructible.

PVC is slightly bendable, making toys practically unbreakable and replacing ceramic figurines on many knick-knack shelves. PVC can be molded into solid PVC figurines. Not all of the toys in this book are made from PVC; some are metal or rubber.

PVC
"ALPHA Critters® ©1987 Lloyd Gilbert Made in China"

DURABILITY

Keeping all of these small toys in a drawer, box, or heap is no problem. I have intentionally put several of the catwoman catmobiles (McD) into the toy box with all the other toys and used a PVC rake to move them back and forth, dump them out, and toss them back and forth, etc. The thin cat's tail of the catmobile which projects out about an inch and a half has never broken off of any of these toys! Even this fragile looking projection seems to be stable and unbreakable. I am sure it would break if one intentionally applied sufficient force, but haphazard stress is withstood. The only mishaps are that some paint seems to wear off of the toys or is scrapped off by rubbing on the floor or sidewalk or a kid chews on the figurine. Another thing to watch is that some of the glued parts do separate: like the figurines on a vehicle, which can easily be repaired.

ENJOY THEM!

Display! Display! Display! With so many small toys being given away, a toy box is not sufficient. We take one shelf and display the entire set for a month. Then we put up a new series with the changing of the calendar page. After seeing Babar for a month, we switch to Matchboxes. To make things more interesting, we choose a theme — like dogs or figures on skateboards. Everybody has to hunt through their collections to contribute something. New collections are set up on another shelf or in a dollhouse/playset for all to enjoy, a new piece is added once a week, more or less, until the set is complete.

Most of the toys stay in mint condition even after being jostled. Cleaning them is a snap: if they are dirty, scrub them with an old toothbrush and scouring powder (Ajax or Comet) and water. Do NOT scrub them if the paint starts peeling! Scrubbing usually gets off all the marks while leaving the paint intact. Ink pen markings will not come off! Ink is absorbed into the plastic PVC. So please do not mark the price or names on the figurines. I thank you.

HOW TO COLLECT

To most collectors, the entire set is desirable to have. Millions, maybe even billions, of each piece are made. A lot of serious collectors only collect premiums that are left in the package — "MIP" or "mint-in-package," figuring the premium will be worth more money if left in the original wrapping. But most collectors want to be able to enjoy their collection.

If you did not get the premium at the restaurant, you can still find most of them at very reasonable prices. Prices for these premiums start as low as a dime or a quarter at yard sales, thrift stores, and flea markets. With this hobby you have to learn patience. And it takes a lot of patient hunting and searching to find them. You have to make a real effort to collect all of the sets every month from the restaurants or digging through toy boxes. There are some harder to find pieces, such as foreign toys. But many vacationers and military families bring back these toys! If you do not have time, there are many dealers who do the leg work for you and offer a good selection at toys shows, etc.

A collection like this is never complete. There are always a few undiscovered toys and more toys coming out every week.

With so many premiums on the market, start off collecting only the things you enjoy. As you find each premium, check it off in this book and make comments about it; such as the price you paid for the premium and where you found it — "bought a kid's meal on 7/20/94, on vacation in Orlando," "best friend had 2 and gave me one," "gave one to cousin Larry," "sold for 25 cents at a yard sale." Include any notes that personalize the collection for you.

Some people only go to one fast food place and collect those toys only. Some people only collect their favorite cartoon characters: only Disney, Hanna-Barbera, or Warner Brothers. Others only collect cars, Barbies, Scooby Doo, dinosaurs, jungle animals, ballerinas, angels, sports figures, sports equipment, surfing figures, flying disks, hamburger items, etc. The list and the combinations are endless and a good collection of many things has already been given away by the restaurants.

This is one hobby anyone can enjoy. Our local TV news station had one favorite toy sitting on a desk behind the newscasters. Shops, banks, secretaries, all have them sitting by cash registers or pencil boxes. Just one of these figurines can brighten up an otherwise dull view or bring a smile to a sick friend. They're not just for kids anymore. Enjoy!

"What a delightful treasure of a book, compounding all those wonderful childhood memories of toys with the joyful reminiscing of happy events spent with those we love during those special time-outs!" ...Sabrina Hawkey, Jacksonville, Florida

CLUBS

Here are some sources that would be of some fun. When writing, include an SASE (self-addressed, stamped envelope) for information about joining the various clubs.

Angel Collectors Club of America
Pauline Neff
2689 Centennial Ct.
Alexandria, VA 22311

Burger King Kid's Club
Main Club House
P.O. Box 1527
Tucker, GA 30085-1527

Disneyana
National Fantasy Fan Club
Box 19212
Irvine, CA 92713

Drinking Glasses Collectors
Collector Glass News
P.O. Box 308
Slippery Rock, PA 16057

Club Lisa Frank
P.O. Box 5586
Tucson, AZ 85703-0586

Fisher Price Collectors Club
Jeanne Kennedy
1442 N. Ogden
Messa, AZ 85703-0586

GI Joe Collectors' Club
Brian Savage
12513 Birchfalls Dr
Raleigh, NC 27614

Holly Hobby Collectibles of America
Helen McCale
PO Box 397
Butler, Mo 64730-0397

LEGO Builders Club
P.O. Box 5000
Unionville, CT 06087-5000

Matchbox International Collectors
Association
Attention: R. Schneider
P.O. Box 28072
Waterloo, Ontario N2L 6J8 Canada
(For info, please enclose, $5)

McDonald's Collector's Club
P.O. Box 633
Joplin, MO 64802

North American Diecast Toy Collectors
Association
Dana Johnson Enterprises
POB 1824
Bend, OR 97709-1824

The Shadow Club
P.O. Box 300728
Fern Park, FL 32730

Smurf Collectors International Club
24 Cabot Rd.
W. Massapequa, NY 11758

Southern California Toy Collectors Club
1760 Termino
Long Beach, CA 90804

Star Trek Newsletter
Moonlight Design
1324 Palms Blvd.
Los Angeles, CA 90291

Toy Car Collectors Club
Peter Foss
33290 West 14 Mile Rd #454
West Bloomfield, Mi 48322

Toy Shop Magazine
700 E. State St.
Iola, WI 54990

ABBREVIATIONS USED IN THIS BOOK

MIP = Mint in Package — the toy comes in its plastic bag with all pieces, parts and papers.

U-3 = toys for children under the age of 3 years old.

* (before the name) = this toy is NOT pictured.

GUIDE TO PHOTO CAPTIONS

Set name and number of items per set.

Toy name with m to keep a checklist of items in your collection.

Restaurant which distributed the toy, year, approximate cost.

Comments, if any.

Identification marks which were cast in the mold with the toy.

UNITED STATES MARKET
FAST FOOD TOYS

7-Eleven & Arby's

Row 1: 7-Eleven:
○ Toy 1: Mini Disk
7-Eleven 1992, $3
Markings: "7-Eleven Slurpee®"
○ Toy 2: Triprong Flyer
7-Eleven 1992, $3
Markings: "7-Eleven (logo)"
○ Toy 3: Mr Big Bite
7-Eleven, $25-30
Mr Big Bite Holding a Slurpee.
Markings: "Mr Big Bite (logo)"
Row 1: Oscar Mayer Hot Dog Whistle-2 per set:
○ Toy 4: With Paper Band
○ Toy 5: With Molded Band
7-Eleven 1990, $3-5 each.
Markings: "Oscar Mayer (logo)"
Row 2: Babar's World Tour Finger Puppets-
4 per set:

○ Toy 1: King Babar
○ Toy 2: Queen Celeste
○ Toy 3: Cousin Arthur & Zephir
○ Toy 4: Pom
Arby's 1990, $3-5 each.
All of Babar Children's books were written by the French
author Laurent de Brunhoff during the 1930s and
translated by Merle Haas.
Markings: "Arby's™ & ©1990 L De Brunhoff Made in
China"
Row 3: Babar's World Tour Racers-3 per set:
○ Toy 1: King Babar
○ Toy 2: Cousin Arthur
○ Toy 3: Queen Celeste
Arby's 1992, $3-5 each.
About 2.25" long.
Markings: "Arby's™ & ©1992 L De Brunhoff Made in
China"

Arby's

Row 1: Babar's World Tour Squirters-3 per set:
❍ Toy 1: King Babar
❍ Toy 2: Cousin Arthur
❍ Toy 3: Queen Celeste
Arby's 1992, $1-3 each.
Water squirters.
Markings: "™ & ©1992 L De Brunhoff Arby's® (logo)
Made in China"
Row 1: Babar's World Tour Stampers-3 per set:
❍ Toy 4: King Babar- "NOW READ THIS"
❍ Toy 5: Zephir- "THIS BOOK BELONGS TO"
❍ Toy 6: Rataxes- "MESSAGE FROM"
Arby's 1991, $3-5 each.
Rubber stampers.
Markings: "™ & ©1991 L De Brunhoff Arby's® (logo)
Made in China"

Row 2: Babar's World Tour Vehicles-3 per set:
❍ Toy 1: King Babar
❍ Toy 2: Zephir
❍ Toy 3: Cousin Arthur
Arby's 1990, $3-5 each.
Markings: "™ & ©1990 L De Brunhoff Arby's® (logo)
Made in China"
Row 3: Crazy Cruisers-Winter Wonderland-
3 per set:
❍ Toy 1: Yogi
❍ Toy 2: Snagglepus
❍ Toy 3: Cindy
Arby's 1994, $3-4 each.
Markings: "©1994 HBPI All Rights Reserved ©1994 Arby's
Inc China"

Arby's

Row 1: Little Miss-8 per set:
○ Toy 1: Little Miss Helpful
○ Toy 2: Little Miss Shy
○ Toy 3: Little Miss Splendid
○ Toy 4: Little Miss Sunshine
○ Toy 5: Little Miss Naughty
○ Toy 6: Little Miss Late
○ Toy 7: Little Miss Lucky
○ Toy 8: Little Miss Giggles
Arby's 1901, $3-5 each.
About 1.5" tall. These plush characters were also sold in stores with tapes and books.
Markings: "Arby's® (logo) ©1981 Hargraves Lic By NEA"
Row 2: Looney Tunes Car-Tunes-6 per set:
○ Toy 1: Sylvester Cat-Illac
○ Toy 2: Bugs Bunny Buggy
○ Toy 3: Tasmanian Devil Slush Musher
○ Toy 4: Road Runner Racer

○ Toy 5: Yosemite Sam Rockin' Frockin' Wagon
○ Toy 6: Daffy Duck Dragster
Arby's 1989, $2-5 each.
These are Warner Brothers characters dating back to the 1930s.
Markings: "Arby's® (logo)™ & ©WB 1989 Made in China"
Row 3: Looney Tunes Fun Figures-3 per set:
○ Toy 1: Fireman Sylvester
○ Toy 2: Freshman Daffy
○ Toy 3: Pilot Taz
Arby's 1989, $3-6 each.
Markings: "©WB 1989 Made in China Arby's® (logo)"
Row 3: Looney Tunes Holiday Figurines-3 per set:
○ Toy 4: Elf Tweety Bird
○ Toy 5: Santa Bugs
○ Toy 6: Toy Soldier Porky
Arby's 1989, $5-7 each.
Markings: "Arby's® (logo)™ & ©WB 1989 Made in China"

Arby's

Row 1: Looney Tunes on Oval Bases-7 per set:
- ○ Toy 1: Pepe Lepew
- ○ Toy 2: Bugs Bunny
- ○ Toy 3: Yosemite Sam
- ○ Toy 4: Sylvester
- ○ Toy 5: Tweety Bird
- ○ Toy 6: Porky Pig
- ○ Toy 7: Tazmanian Devil

Arby's 1987, $3-5 each.
About 2" tall.
Markings: "Arby's® (logo) ©Warner Brothers Inc 1987"

Row 2: Looney Tunes Pencil Toppers-6 per set:
- ○ Toy 1: Sylvester
- ○ Toy 2: Daffy Duck
- ○ Toy 3: Taz
- ○ Also: Yosemite Sam, Porky, and Tweety

Arby's 1988, $4-5 each.
Pencil topper about 1.5" tall.
Markings: "Arby's® (logo) ©WB 1988"

Row 3: Looney Tunes Straight Legged Characters- 6 per set:
- ○ Toy 1: Tazmanian Devil
- ○ Toy 2: Elmer Fudd
- ○ Toy 3: Road Runner
- ○ Toy 4: Bugs Bunny
- ○ Toy 5: Daffy Duck
- ○ Toy 6: Wilie E Coyote

Arby's 1988, $4-5 each.
Markings: "©WB 1988 Arby's® (logo)"

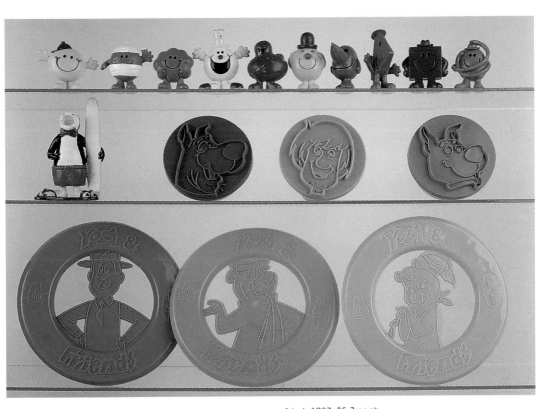

Arby's

Row 1: Mr Men-10 per set:
- ◯ Toy 1: Mr Bounce
- ◯ Toy 2: Mr Bump
- ◯ Toy 3: Mr Daydream
- ◯ Toy 4: Mr Funny
- ◯ Toy 5: Mr Greedy
- ◯ Toy 6: Mr Mischief
- ◯ Toy 7: Mr Nosey
- ◯ Toy 8: Mr Rush
- ◯ Toy 9: Mr Strong
- ◯ Toy 10: Mr Tickle

Arby's 1981, $3-6 each.
About 1.5 to 2" tall. Plush characters, tapes and books were sold in stores.
Markings: "Hargraves Lic by NEA ©1981 Arby's® (logo)"

Row 2: Polar Swirl Penguins-5 per set:
- ◯ Toy 1: Surfer
- ◯ Also: Snorkler, With Walkman, Wearing yellow shorts, and wearing blue shorts

Arby's 1987, $5-7 each.
Same penguin dressed in different outfits.
Markings: "Arby's® (logo) China"

Row 2: Scooby Doo Dough-3 per set:
- ◯ Toy 2: Scooby Doo
- ◯ Toy 3: Shaggy
- ◯ Toy 4: Scrappy Doo

Arby's 1994, $2 each.
TV cartoon by Hanna-Barbera.
Markings: "Made in China" Sticker: "©1994 HBPI Arby's® (logo) ©1994 Arby's Inc"

Row 3: Yogi & Friends Mini Disks-4 per set:
- ◯ Toy 1: Ranger Smith
- ◯ Toy 2: Yogi
- ◯ Toy 3: Cindy
- ◯ Also: Snagglepus

Arby's 1993, $1-2 each.
About 6" diameter.
Markings: "©1993 Arby's Inc ©1993 Hanna-Barbera Productions Inc All Rights Reserved:

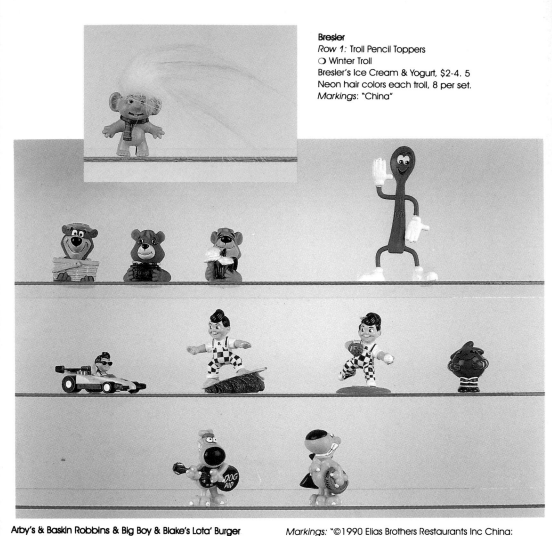

Arby's & Baskin Robbins & Big Boy & Blake's Lota' Burger
Row 1: Yogi & Friends Squirters-3 per set:
❍ Toy 1: Yogi Bear
❍ Toy 2: Cindy Bear
❍ Toy 3: Boo-Boo Bear
Arby's 1994, $2-4 each.
Water squirters.
Markings: "©HBPI ©1994 Arby's Inc China"
Row 1: Pinkie the Spoon
❍ Toy 4: Pinkie the Spoon
Baskin Robbins 1991, $12-16.
Markings: "Baskin 31 Robbins (logo)"
Row 2: Big Boy Sports Figures-4 per set:
❍ Toy 1: Big Boy in Racing Car
❍ Toy 2: Big Boy Surfing
❍ Toy 3: Big Boy playing Baseball
❍ Also: Big Boy Roller Skating
Big Boy Restaurants/Elias Brothers Restaurants 1990, $3-6 each.

Markings: "©1990 Elias Brothers Restaurants Inc China:
Row 2: Play Yard
❍ Toy 4: Blueberry
❍ Also: Strawberry, Grape, Sandbox, Slide,
        Swing, and Teeter-Totter
Big Boy Restaurants 1992, $5-10 each.
This was a play set with fruit "people".
Markings: "©1991 Bang a Drum Ent Mfg by Procorp Inc"
Row 3: Grimmy-6 per set:
❍ Toy 1: Dog Aid
❍ Toy 2: Dog Food
❍ Also: "Fleas on Board (sign)" Sitting, Leash,
        and with Open Arms
Blake's Lota' Burger 1989, $5-12 each.
Also sold retail.
Markings: "™ & ©1989 Grimmy Inc Lic by MGM/UA 1989 DCN Ind Inc"

Burger King

Row 1: Aladdin-5 per set:
- ○ Toy 1: Aladdin on the Magic Carpet
- ○ Toy 2: Princess Jasmine on Raja the Tiger
- ○ Toy 3: Jafar the Sorcerer
- ○ Toy 4: Genie in the Lamp
- ○ Toy 5: Abu the Monkey

Burger King 1992, $4-5 each.
A Disney cartoon motion picture.
Markings: "©Disney Mfg for Burger King Corp China"

Row 2: Archie Comics-4 per set:
- ○ Toy 1: Archie in Red Jalopie
- ○ Toy 2: Betty in '57 Chevy
- ○ Toy 3: Veronica in Corvette
- ○ Toy 4: Jughead in VW Bug

Burger King 1991, $4-5 each.
Comic book characters from the 1940s.
Markings: "©1991 Archie Comic Pub Inc® 1990 General Motors Corp Made in China Burger King Kid's Club (logo)"

Row 3: Barnyard Commando Cuffs 4 per set:
- ○ Toy 1: Major Leggar Mutton
- ○ Toy 2: Sergeant Short 'n' Sweet
- ○ Toy 3: Sergeant Woolly Pullover
- ○ Toy 4: Private Side o' Bacon

Burger King 1990, $2-5 each.
TV cartoons, PVC bracelets.
Markings: "Made in China™ ©TCFC Mfg for Burger King Corp"

Row 4: Beauty & the Beast-4 per set:
- ○ Toy 1: Beast
- ○ Toy 2: Belle
- ○ Toy 3: Chip
- ○ Toy 4: Cogsworth

Burger King 1992, $2-3 each.
A Disney cartoon motion picture.
Markings: "©Disney China Mfg for Burger King"

17

Burger King

Row 1: Beetlejuice-6 per set:

○ Toy 1: The Uneasy Chair—BJ/Charles

○ Toy 2: The Charmer-BJ/BJ

○ Toy 3: The Ghost Host—BJ/BJ, Lydia, Delia, Charles

○ Toy 4: Peek-A-Boo-Boo—BJ/Delia

○ Toy 5: Ghost-to-Ghost TV—BJ/Jacques

○ Toy 6: Head Over Heals—BJ/Lydia

Burger King 1990, $3-4 each.

TV cartoons, two-sided to show BJ/other BJ cartoon characters.

Markings: "Made in China"

Row 2: Bone Age-4 per set:

○ Toy 1: Fangra™

○ Toy 2: T Rex™

○ Toy 3: Mastus™

○ Toy 4: Deitron™

Burger King 1988, $4-5 each.

Movable heads and tails.

Markings: "©Kenner 1989"

Row 3: Bonkers-5 per set:

○ Toy 1: Fall-Apart Rabbit

○ Toy 2: Jitters

○ Toy 3: Toots

○ Toy 4: Piquel

○ Toy 5: Bonkers

Burger King 1993, $3-4 each.

TV cartoon series, cars some in three sections each plus driver, bottoms do not mix or match different car pieces.

Markings: "Burger King Kid's Club (logo) ©Disney Mfg for Burger King Corp Made in China"

Row 4: Burger King Action Figures-4/5 per set:

○ Toy 1: IQ

○ Toy 2: Jaws

○ Toy 3: Kid Vid

○ Toy 4: Boomer-also came with blue skates and brown gloves

Burger King 1992, $3-4 each.

Burger King's characters.

Markings: "©1990 Burger King Corp China"

Burger King

Row 1: Burger King All Stars Sports Kids-
5 per set:
○ Toy 1: Jaws-Football
○ Toy 2: Boomer-Ice Hockey
○ Toy 3: Kid Vid- Basketball
Row 2:
○ Toy 4: IQ-Disk Throwing
○ Toy 5: Snaps-Soccer
Burger King 1994, $2-3 each.
Three pieces each.
Markings: all pieces with "Burger King"
Row 3: Burger King Glow-in-the-Dark Trolls-
4 per set:
○ Toy 1: IQ Troll

○ Toy 2: Kid Vid Troll
○ Toy 3: Snaps Troll
○ Toy 4: Jaws Troll
Burger King 1993, $3-5 each.
Burger King characters turned into trolls!
Markings: "Burger King Kid's Club (logo) ©1993 Burger
King Corp Made in China"
Row 4: Burger King It's Magic-4 per set:
○ Toy 1: Snaps' Magic Frame
○ Toy 2: Jaws Disappearing Food
○ Toy 3: IQ's Magic Trunk
○ Toy 4: Kid Vid's Disappearing Act
Burger King 1992, $3-4 each.
Markings: "Burger King Kid's Club (logo) ©1992 Burger
King Corporation Made in China"

Burger King

Row 1: Burger King Kid Transporters-6 per set:
- Toy 1: IQ in World Bookmobile
- Toy 2: Boomer in Super Shoe
- Toy 3: Kid Vid in Sega Video Gamester
- Toy 4: Wheelie in Turbo Wheelchair

Row 2:
- Toy 5: Snaps in Camera Car
- Toy 6: Jaws in Burger Racer

Burger King 1990, $4-5 each.
Two pieces each.

Markings: "©1990 Burger King Corp China"

Row 3: Burger King Pranks-5 per set:
- Toy 1: Lingo's Snake-3 pieces
- Toy 2: Jaws' Giant Spider
- Toy 3: Boomer's Buzzer

Row 4:
- Toy 4: IQ's Woopee Cushion-folded
- Toy 5: Kid Vid's RC Squirter

Burger King 1994, $2-3 each.
Markings: "Burger King Kid's Club (logo) ©1993 Burger King Corporation Made in China"

Burger King

Row 1: Burger King Top Kids-4 per set:
- ○ Toy 1: Kid Vid
- ○ Toy 2: Wheelie
- ○ Toy 3: Jaws
- ○ Toy 4: Boomer

Burger King 1993, $2-3 each.
Bottom spins off as a "top."
Markings: "©1992 Burger King Corp Made in China"
Rows 2 & 3: Burger King Water Mates-4 per set:
- ○ Toy 1: IQ on Dolphin
- ○ Toy 2: Snaps in a Glass Row Boat-2 pieces
- ○ Toy 3: Lingo on a Jet Ski
- ○ Toy 4: Kid Vid on a Raft-2 pieces

Burger King 1991, $2-4 each.
Each Kid came in two different colors as shown on the two separate shelves.
Markings: "©1990 Burger King Corp China".
Row 4: Capitol Critters-4 per set:
- ○ Toy 1: Muggle in Lincoln's Armchair
- ○ Toy 2: Jammet Jams at the White House
- ○ Toy 3: Max Cleans up with Jefferson
- ○ Toy 4: Presidential Cat Spies on the Good Guys

Burger King 1992, $3-4 each.
A short lived summer TV prime time cartoon.
Markings: "™ & ©92 SBP Made in China Burger King Kids Club (logo)"

Burger King

Row 1: Captain Planet-4 per set:
- ○ Toy 1: Captain Planet/Hoggish Greedily
- ○ Toy 2: Duke Nukum/Wheeler
- ○ Toy 3: Dr Blight/Mati & Linka
- ○ Toy 4: Gee & Quami/Sludge-2 pieces

Burger King 1990, $2-4 each.
TV cartoons, cars flip over to reveal heroes/villains.

Markings: "©1990 TBS Prod & DIC Enter Mfg for Burger King China"
Row 2: Dino Crawlers-5 per set:
- ○ Toys 1-5: No names

Burger King 1993, $2-3 each.
Wind-ups.
Markings: "Made in China Burger King Kid's Club (logo)"

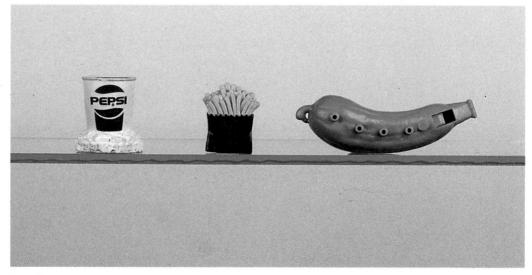

Burger King

Row 1: Fast Food Miniatures-5 per set:
- ○ Toy 1: Pepsi
- ○ Toy 2: Fries
- ○ Also: Burger King Package Fries, Hot Dog, and Whopper

Burger King 1983, $6-10 each.

About 1.75" tall.
Markings: "Russ China"
Row 1: Fun Food
- ○ Toy 3: Pickle-O

Burger King, $6-8.
Whistle or musical instrument.
Markings: "Burger King (logo)"

Burger King

Row 1: Gargoyles-4 per set:
○ Toy 1: Color Transformation Cup
○ Toy 2: Color Mutation "Broadway"
○ Toy 3: Spin to Life "Goliath"
○ Toy 4: Gargoyles Pop-Up book
Burger King 1995, $3-5 each.
A TV cartoon series.
Markings: "Mfg for Burger King Corp Made in China ©BVTV"

Row 2: Go-Go Gadget Gizmos-4 per set:
○ Toy 1: Copter Gadget-3 pieces
○ Toy 2: Inflated Gadget
○ Toy 3: Scuba Gadget
○ Toy 4: Surfer Gadget-3 pieces
Burger King 1991, $4-5 each.
TV cartoons.
Markings: "©1991 DIC China Mfg for Burger King®"

Row 3: Good Goblin'-3 per set:
○ Toy 1: Frankie Steen
○ Toy 2: Zelda Zoombroom
○ Toy 3: Gordy Goblin
Burger King 1989, $5-6 each.
Three pieces each.
Markings: "©1989 Burger King Corporation Made in China"

Burger King

Row 1: Goof Troup Bowlers- 4 per set:
- ○ Toy 1: Goofy
- ○ Toy 2: Pete
- ○ Toy 3: PJ
- ○ Toy 4: Max

Burger King 1992, $2-4 each.
Disney TV cartoon series.
Markings: "Burger King Kids Club (logo) ©Disney Made in China"

Row 2: Goofy Movie-5 per set:
- ○ Toy 1: Goofy & Max in Water Raft-squirter
- ○ Toy 2: Goofy & Max on Water Skis
- ○ Toy 3: Goofy on Bucking Bronco
- ○ Toy 4: Goofy & Max in Fishing Boat
- ○ Toy 5: Goofy & Max in Runaway Car

Burger King 1995, $2-3 each.
A Disney cartoon motion picture.
Markings: "Burger King Kids Club (logo) ©Disney Mfg for Burger King Corp China"

Row 3: King Burger-2 per set:
- ○ Toy 1: King Burger Pencil Topper
- ○ Toy 2: King Burger Mini-disk

Burger King 1979, $10-15 each.
About 2" tall.
Markings: "©1979 Burger King Corporation"

Burger King

Row 1: Lickety Splits Rolling Racers
- ○ Toy 1: Carbo Cooler
- ○ Toy 2: Carsan'wich
- ○ Toy 3; Chicken Chassis
- ○ Toy 4: Expresstix
- ○ Toy 5: Flame Broiled Buggy
- ○ Toy 6: Indianapolis Racer
- ○ Toy 7: Spry Fries

Burger King 1989, $1-3 each.
Markings: "©1989 Hallmark Cards Inc" or "©1989 Graphics Int'l Inc Made in China"

Row 2: Life Saver Freaky Fellas-4 per set:
- ○ Toys 1-4 No names-2 pieces each

Burger King 1991, $2-4 each.
PVC critter holds roll of Life Savers.
Markings: "©1991 Burger King Corporation Made in China"

Row 3: Lion King-7 per set:
- ○ Toy 1: Mufasa
- ○ Toy 2: Young Nala
- ○ Toy 3: Young Simba
- ○ Toy 4: Scar
- ○ Toy 5: Rafiki
- ○ Toy 6: Ed the Hyena
- ○ Toy 7: Pumbaa & Timon

Burger King 1994, $4-6 each.
A Disney cartoon motion picture.
Markings: "©Disney Mfg for Burger King Corp Made in China"

Row 4: Lion King Finger Puppets 6 per set:
- ○ Toy 1: Pumbaa
- ○ Toy 2: Rafiki
- ○ Toy 3: Simba
- ○ Toy 4: Ed
- ○ Toy 5: Mufasa
- ○ Toy 6: Scar

Burger King 1995, $3-4 each.
Finger puppets in pop-up boxes.
Markings: "©Disney Made in China Mfg for Burger King Corp"

Burger King

Row 1: Little Mermaid Splash Collection- ·
4 per set:
- ⭕ Toy 1: Ariel on Wind-Up Sea Turtle-2 pieces
- ⭕ Toy 2: Flounder-squirter, has Burger King Kid's
    Club logo
- ⭕ Toy 3: Sebastian Wind-Up
- ⭕ Toy 4: Urchin Squirt Toy-squirter

Burger King 1993, $3-4 each.
A Disney cartoon motion picture & TV series. Little
Mermaid was also distributed by McDonald's.
Markings: "©Disney Made in China Burger King Kid's Club
(logo)"
Row 2: Matchbox Cars-4 per set:
- ⭕ Toy 1: 4x4 Mountain Man
- ⭕ Also: Ferrari (red), Ford LTD Police Car, and
    Corvette (yellow)

Burger King 1987, $5-7 each.
Markings: "Matchbox (logo) Mini Pick up Matchbox Toys

Made in Macau"
Row 2: Mickey's Toontown Disneyland-
4 per set:
- ⭕ Toy 2: Mickey & Minnie
- ⭕ Toy 3: Goofy
- ⭕ Toy 4: Donald
- ⭕ Toy 5: Chip 'n' Dale

Burger King 1991, $3-5 each.
Wind-ups.
Markings: "©Disney Mfg for Burger King Corp China
Burger King Kid's Club (logo)"
Row 3: Mini Sports Games-4 per set:
- ⭕ Toy 1: Catch mitt with Ball-4.5"
- ⭕ Toy 2: Football-4"
- ⭕ Toy 3: Basketball-1.5" diameter
- ⭕ Toy 4: Inflatable Soccer Ball-8" diameter

Burger King 1993, $2 each.
Markings: "©1993 Burger King Corp China"

Burger King

Row 1: Nerfuls-4 per set:

○ Toy 1: Officer Bob
○ Toy 2: Bitsy Ball
○ Toy 3: Fetch
○ Toy 4: Scratch

Burger King 1989, $4-5 each.

Three pieces each: a face ball that came with a suit and a hat or hair. The Nerfuls also sold in stores with roundish houses, cars, furniture, play swings etc.

Markings: "©1985 PB Parker Brothers"

Row 2: Nightmare Before Christmas Watches-4 per set:

○ Toy 1: Christmastown
○ Toy 2: Pumpkins
○ Toy 3: Bats & Cats
○ Toy 4: Halloweentown

Burger King 1993, $5-6 each. Watches.

Markings: "©Touchstone Pictures"

Row 3: Purr-Tenders-4 per set:

○ Toy 1: Scamp-purr on Cheese
○ Toy 2: Romp-purr, Hop-purr, & Flop-purr in Flip Car
○ Toy 3: (same car-cats flipped over)
○ Toy 4: Hop-purr on Radio-Bank
○ Also: Book

Burger King 1988, $6-8 each.

Burger King also had plush Purr-Tenders (*see Plush & Big*)

Markings: "©1988 Burger King Corp ©1987 Hallmark Cards Inc Designed by Linda Breitel/Cliff Rosenberg

Row 4: Record Breakers-6 per set:

○ Toy 1: Accelerator
○ Toy 2: Shockwave
○ Toy 3: Fastlane
○ Toy 4: Aero
○ Toy 5: Indy
○ Toy 6: Dominator

Burger King 1990, 4-5 each.

Markings: "©1989 Hasbro All Rights Reserved 1989 Mfg for Burger King Corporation Made in China"

Burger King

Row 1: Silverhawks-1 figurine:
○ Toy 1: Silverhawks Pencil Topper
Burger King 1987, $8-10 each.
A TV cartoon.
Markings: "©1987 Telepix"
Row 1: Simpsons-5 per set:
○ Toy 2: Homer
○ Toy 3: Marge
○ Toy 4: Bart
○ Toy 5: Lisa
○ Toy 6: Maggie
Burger King 1989, $3-4 each.
Prime Time TV cartoon series. Burger King also sold plush
Simpson's characters (*see Plush & Big*).
Markings: "Made in China TM & ©1990 TCFFC"
Row 2: Spacebase Racers-4 per set:
○ Toy 1: Cosmic Copter
○ Toy 2: Moonman Rover
○ Toy 3: Starship Viking
○ Toy 4: Super Shuttle
Burger King 1989, $6-8 each.
Markings: "©1989 Burger King Corporation Made in
China"

Row 3: Super Powers-1 figurine:
○ Toy 1: Aquaman
Burger King 1987, $15-20.
Markings: "©DC 1988"
Row 3: Super Powers Cup Holder-4 per set:
○ Toy 2: Darkseid
○ Also: Wonder Woman, Batman, & Superman
Burger King 1988, $12-15 each.
Figurines hold a white drinking cup.
Markings: "Darkseid is a Trademark of DC Comics Inc
©1988 Figurine Cupholder Created by Robert Demars
Pat Pend"
Row 3: Teenage Mutant Ninja Turtles Bike Gear-
5 per set:
○ Toy 3: Water Bottle
Row 4:
○ Toy 1: Pouch
○ Toy 2: Horn
○ Toy 3: Spike Buttons
○ Toy 4: License Plates
Burger King 1991, $2-4 each.
A TV cartoon series and a motion picture.
Markings: "Burger King Kid's Club (logo) ©Mirage Studios
Made in China"

Burger King

Row 1: Pocahontas-8 per set:
○ Toy 1: John Smith
○ Toy 2: Meeko
○ Also: Pocahontas, Grandmother Willow,
　　　　Governor Ratcliffe, Chief Powhatan,
　　Flit, and Percy
Burger King 1995, $3-5 each.
Markings: "©Disney Mfg for Burger King Corp China"

Burger King

Row 1: Teenage Mutant Ninja Turtles Rad Badges-
6 per set:
○ Toy 1: Heroes in a Half Shell
○ Toy 2: Raphael
○ Toy 3: Leonardo
○ Toy 4: Donatello
Row 2:
○ Toy 5: Michaelangelo
○ Toy 6: Shredder
Burger King 1989, $5-6 each.
With suction cups.
Markings: "Mfg for Burger King Corp 1989 Excl Lic by
Surge Licensing ©Mirage Studios 1989"
Row 3: Thundercats-1 figurine:
○ Toy 1: Snarf Straw Holder
Burger King 1986, $5-6.
TV cartoons.
Markings: "©1986 TPXLCI T WOLF"

Row 3: Walt Disney World-4 per set:
○ Toy 2: Mickey
○ Toy 3: Minnie
○ Toy 4: Donald Duck
○ Toy 5: Roger Rabbit
Burger King 1993, $2-4 each.
Wind-Ups, came with a parade track for the 20th
anniversary for Disney World.
Markings: "©Disney Mfg for Burger King Corp China"
Row 4: Z-Bots-5 per set:
○ Toy 1: Buzzsaw
○ Toy 2: Jawbreaker
○ Toy 3: Turbine
○ Toy 4: Skyviper
○ Toy 5: Bugeye
Burger King 1994, $2-4 each.
Also came with four pogs each.
Markings: "©1993 LGTI BK China"

Carl's Jr

Row 1: Bone A Fide Friends-4 per set:
○ Toy 1: "Steggly"
○ Toy 2: "Donney"
○ Toy 3: "Ty"
○ Toy 4: "Topsy"
Carl's Jr 1994, $4-6 each.
Dino skin "costumes" come off to reveal the skeletons, three pieces each.
Markings: "Carl's Jr® 1994 China"
Row 2: Camp California-4 per set:
○ Toy 1: Bear Squirter-squirter
○ Toy 2: Lil' Bro Disk
○ Toy 3: Mini Volleyball
○ Toy 4: Spinner

Carl's Jr 1992, $2-5 each.
Similar set distributed by Hardee's.
Markings: "Carl Karcher Ent ©92 Camp Cal China"
Row 3 & Row 4: Fun House Faces-6 per set:
○ Toy 1: Rudy Rabbit
○ Toy 2: Barney Bear
○ Toy 3: Petey Pumpkin
○ Toy 4: Glenda Ghost
○ Toy 5: Franklin
○ Toy 6: Tina Tiger
Carl's Jr 1990, $2-5 each.
You insert four fingertips into the back to move the mask.
Markings: "Carl's Jr (logo) ©Carl Karchen Enterprises Inc 1990 Made in China"

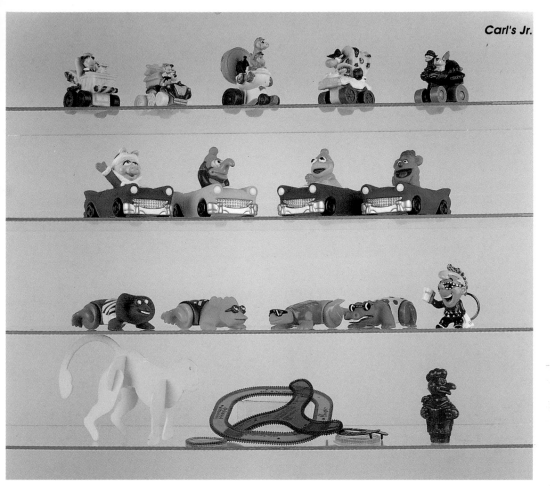

Carl's Jr & Checkers & Chick-Fil-A

Row 1: Fender Bender 500-5 per set:
○ Toy 1: Yogi & Boo Boo in Jellystone Jammer
○ Toy 2: Huckleberry Hound & Snagglepuss in
　　　　Lucky Trucky
○ Toy 3: Magilla Gorilla & Wally Gator in
　　　　Swamp Stomper
○ Toy 4: Dick Dastardly & Muttley in Dirty
　　　　Truckster
○ Toy 5: Quick Draw McGraw & Baba Looey in
　　　　Texas Twister
Carl's Jr 1990, $5-6 each.
Also distributed by Hardee's. TV cartoon series by Hanna-Barbera.
Markings: "©1990 H-B Prod Inc Lic by HPI China"
Row 2: Muppet Parade of Stars-4 per set:
○ Toy 1: Miss Piggy
○ Toy 2: Gonzo
○ Toy 3: Kermit
○ Toy 4: Fozzie
Carl's Jr 1992, $5-6 each.
Two pieces each-the characters are finger puppets
which fit onto projection in car seat.
Markings: characters only: "©Henson China"
Row 3: Raging Reptiles-4 per set:
○ Toys 1-4: no names

Carl's Jr 1994, $3-4 each.
No Markings, Printed: "Carl's Jr® Made in China"
Row 3: Checkers-1 figurine:
○ Toy 5: Checkers Key Chain
Checkers Drive-In 1993, $5-7.
No kid's meal premiums, this key chain is sold separately
and worthwhile collecting.
Markings: "China"
Row 4: African Animals-8 per set:
○ Toy 1: Monkey
○ Also: Elephant, Lion, Hippo, Water Buffalo, Ostrich,
　　　　Zebra, and Giraffe
Chick-Fil-A 1991, $3-5 each.
Animal Puzzles, also distributed by McDonald's Canada.
Markings: "Chick-Fil-A® (logo)"
Row 4: Doodles Doodlers:
○ Drawing Tools-multipieces each-2 sets shown here
Chick-Fil-A 1994, $3-4 each.
Markings: "Chick-Fil-A® (logo) Chick-Fil-A Inc® 1994
Doodles® Doodlers ©Namkung Taiwan"
Row 4: Pencil Topper:
○ Toy 3: Chick-Fil-A Pencil Topper
Chick-Fil-A 1992, $3-4.
Markings: "Chick-Fil-A Inc® 1992 ©Namkung 1992
Taiwan"

31

Chick-Fil-A & Dairy Queen

Row 1: Dino Puzzles-6 per set:
○ Toy 1: Bronto
○ Toy 2: Stego
○ Also: 4 others
Chick-Fil-A 1993, $3-4 each.
Puzzles.
Markings: "Chick-Fil-A® (logo)"
Row 1: A Farm Puzzle-7 per set:
○ Toy 3: Goat
○ Also: Cow, Horse Pig, Sheep, Farmer, and
    Tractor
Chick-Fil-A 1992, $3-4 each.
Puzzles.
Markings: "Chick-Fil-A® (logo)"
Row 2: Richard Scarry Molds-5 per set:
○ Toy 1: Lowly Worm™
○ Toy 2: Mr Fumble™
○ Toy 3: Heckle Cat™
○ Toy 4: Sergeant Murphy™

○ Also: Hilda Hippo™
Chick-Fil-A 1993, $3-5 each.
Playdough or sand molds.
Markings: "©1993 R Scarry Chick-Fil-A®"
Row 3: Balance Buddies:
  ○ Toy 1-5: 1set of Balance Buddies-5 pieces
Dairy Queen 1994, $2-3.
Stacking Circus figures, also distributed by McDonald's.
No Markings
Row 4: Bear Water Color Set:
○ Toy 1: Bear Water Color Set
Dairy Queen 1993, $2-3.
About 5" tall, water colors are on a palette in the bear case.
Markings: "Made in China"
Row 4: Bloom Ball:
○ Toy 2: Bloom Ball
Dairy Queen 1994, $1-3.
About 2.5" diameter.
No Markings

Dairy Queen
Row 1: Circus Train
❍ Toy 1: Engine
❍ Toy 2: Car/Cage
❍ Toy 3: Car/Cage
❍ Toy 4: Caboose
Dairy Queen 1994, $5-6 each.
Peel-off stickers for each window, pieces attach together.
Markings: "Made in China"
Row 2: Creative Child Cards-4 per set:
❍ Toy 1: ABC Flash Cards
❍ Toy 2: Crazy Eights
❍ Toy 3: Fish
❍ Toy 4: Old Maid
Dairy Queen 1993, $2-3 each.
Playing Cards, also distributed by Hardee's.
Row 3: Dairy Queen Toys-4 per set:
❍ Toy 1: Dinosaur Bubbler

❍ Toy 2: Yo-Yo
❍ Also: Spinner & Book
Dairy Queen 1994, $1-3 each.
Different dinosaurs on the bubbler.
Markings: " ©1992 Dorda Ind Ltd Made in China"
Row 3: Dennis Deck:
❍ Toy 3: Dennis Deck Playing Cards
Dairy Queen 1994, $4-5.
Printed: "® Am DQ Corp ©Am DQ Corp Hank Ketcham
Enterprises Inc"
Row 4: Dennis The Menace-4 per set:
❍ Toy 1: Dennis in Fire Truck
❍ Toy 2: Margaret in Astronaut's suit-3 pieces
❍ Toy 3: Ruff in Dino costume-3 pieces
❍ Toy 4: Joey in #7 Race Car
Dairy Queen 1994, $5-6 each.
Markings: "©Katcham Made in China"

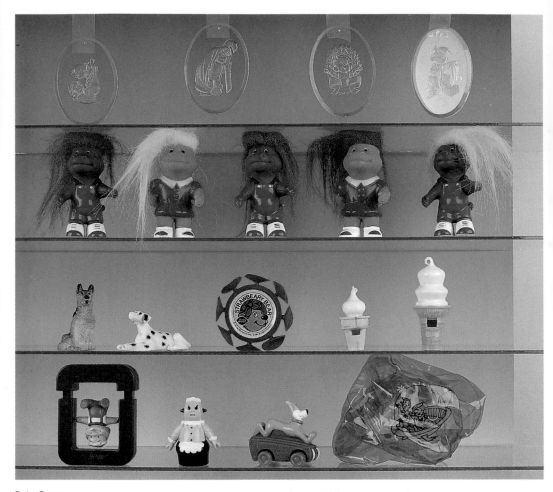

Dairy Queen

Row 1: Dennis The Menace Christmas Ornaments
❍ Toy 1: Dennis with Joey in Stocking
❍ Toy 2: Dennis with Candy Cane
❍ Toy 3: Dennis with Wreath
❍ Toy 4: Dennis Wrapping Gifts
Dairy Queen 1994, $3-4 each.
Markings: "® Ketcham"
Row 2: Dinosaur Trolls:
❍ Toys 1-5: No names-Boys & Girls
Dairy Queen 1993, $3-4 each.
Boy and Girl Dinos with four different colors of hair
"Collect them all."
Markings: "China"
Row 3: Dogs:
❍ Toy 1: German Shepherd
❍ Toy 2: Dalmatian
❍ Also: Others
Dairy Queen 1995, $2-3 each.
Markings: dog name and "China"

Row 3: DQ Spinners-4 per set:
❍ Toy 3: Strawberry Bear
❍ Also: Butterscotch Beaver, Chocolate Chimp,
        and Marshmallow Moose
Dairy Queen 1992, $3-4 each.
Markings: "©CDM 1992 China"
Row 3: Funbunch-2 per set:
❍ Toy 4: Single Ice Cream Cone Whistle
❍ Toy 5: Double Ice Cream Cone Whistle
Dairy Queen 1991, $4-5 each.
Markings: "Dairy Queen DQ Canada"
Row 4: The Jetsons-4 per set:
❍ Toy 1: Elroy's™ Intergalactic Twirler
❍ Toy 2: Rolling Rosie™
❍ Toy 3: Astro's™ Treadmill Workout
❍ Toy 4: George & Jane's™ Space Sphere
Dairy Queen 1995, $4-5 each.
Inflatable Space Sphere is about 7" in diameter-shown
deflated.
Markings: "The Jetsons™ (logo) ©1995 HBPI China"

Dairy Queen

Row 1: Kid's Pick-nic!-4 per set:
○ Toy 1: Puppy in My Pocket™-2 pieces
○ Toy 2: GI Joe™
○ Toy 3: Transformers® Robots in Disguise
○ Toy 4: Kitty Surprise® -2 pieces
Dairy Queen 1995, $2-5 each.
Markings: "Puppy in My Pocket™ ©1994 Morrison
Entertainment Group Inc"
Row 2: Mix and Match Dinosaurs-4 per set:
○ Toy 1: Brontosaurus
○ Toy 2: Pteradactyl
○ Toy 3: Tyranosaurus Rex
○ Toy 4: Stegosaurus
Dairy Queen 1993, $3-5 each.
Also given out by White Castle and Carl's Jr.
No Markings
Row 3: Number Transformers-10 per set:
○ Toy 1: Number 3
○ Also:all numbers from 1 to 10
Dairy Queen 1993, $2-5 each.

Number blocks transform into robots.
No Markings
Row 3: Pullback Racers-6 per set:
○ Toy 2: Bee
○ Toy 3: 3 Stacked Doves
○ Toy 4: Tire with Wings
○ Toy 5: Chevy logo with 4 Stars
○ Toy 6: Flame
○ Also: one other
Dairy Queen 1993, $3-5 each.
2" long each in various colors with different decals on
hood of racer.
Markings: "Made in China"
Decal: "Dairy Queen"
Row 4: Radio Flyer
○ Toy 1: Radio Flyer Wagon
Dairy Queen 1991, $4-5 each.
About 4" long plus handle.
No Markings.
Decals: "Dairy Queen" and "Radio Flyer"

Dairy Queen

Row 1: Rock-A-Doodle-6 per set:
○ Toy 1: Chanticleer
○ Toy 2: Patou
○ Toy 3: Edmund
○ Toy 4: Peepers
○ Toy 5: The Grand Duke of Owl
○ Toy 6: Sniper
Dairy Queen 1992, $7-8 each.
A human-and-cartoon motion picture.
Markings: "™ ©1992 Goldcrest Animation Ltd Made in China"
Row 2: Space Shuttle-4 per set:
○ Toys 1-4: Space Shuttle

Dairy Queen 1993, $3-4 each.
Same model in different colors with different decals.
Markings: "ST® (logo) Copyright Pat Pending Made in China"
Row 3: Tom & Jerry-6 per set:
○ Toy 1 Tom-squirter
○ Toy 2: Tom-stamper
○ Toy 3: Tom in Sports Car
○ Toy 4: Jerry in Sports Car
○ Toy 5: Jerry-stamper
○ Toy 6: Jerry-squirter
Dairy Queen 1993, $3-5 each.
Markings: "©1993 TEC Made in China"

Denny's
Row 1: Denny's Stencils
◯ Toy 1: The Jetsons
◯ Toy 2: Sealife
Denny's, $2-3 each.
Markings: "Denny's® (logo)"
Row 2: Flintstones Dino-Makers-6 per set:
◯ Toy 1: Tyranosaurus Rex
◯ Toy 2: Triceratops
◯ Toy 3: Pteradactyl
◯ Toy 4: Stegosaurus
◯ Toy 5: Brontosaurus
◯ Toy 6: Mastodon
Denny's 1991, $4-5 each.
Two or three parts pop together to let sections turn or twist.
Markings: "Denny's® ©1991 H-B Prod Inc Lic by HPI Made in China"
Row 3: Flintstones Dino-Racers-6 per set:
◯ Toy 1: Pebbles

◯ Toy 2: Fred
◯ Toy 3: Dino
◯ Toy 4: Betty
◯ Toy 5: Barney
◯ Toy 6: Bamm-Bamm
Denny's 1991, $4-5 each.
Markings: "Denny's® ©1991 H-B Prod Inc Lic by HPI Made in China"
Row 4: Flintstones Fun Squirters-6 per set:
◯ Toy 1: Fred
◯ Toy 2: Wilma
◯ Toy 3: Bamm-Bamm
◯ Toy 4: Dino
◯ Toy 5: Barney
◯ Toy 6: Pebbles
Denny's 1991, $3-4 each.
Squirters.
Markings: "Denny's® ©1991 H-B Prod Inc Lic by HPI Made in China"

Denny's

Denny's

Row 1: Flintstones Rock & Rollers-6 per set:
- ❍ Toy 1: Fred
- ❍ Toy 2: Dino
- ❍ Toy 3: Bamm-Bamm
- ❍ Toy 4: Mastodon
- ❍ Toy 5: Barney
- ❍ Toy 6: Pebbles

Denny's 1991, $4-5 each.
Markings: "©1991 H-B Prod Inc Denny's® China Lic by HPI"

Row 2: Flintstones Glacier Gliders-6 per set:
- ❍ Toy 1: Pebbles
- ❍ Toy 2: Barney
- ❍ Toy 3: Fred
- ❍ Toy 4: Bamm-Bamm
- ❍ Toy 5: Hoppy
- ❍ Toy 6: Dino

Denny's 1990, $4-5 each.
Markings: "©1990 Hanna-Barbera Prod Inc Lic by

Hamilton Projects Inc Mfg by Irvine Ca Made in China"
Row 3: Flintstone Stone Age Cruisers-6 per set:
- ❍ Toy 1: Fred
- ❍ Toy 2: Barney
- ❍ Toy 3: Bamm-Bamm
- ❍ Toy 4: Dino
- ❍ Toy 5: Wilma
- ❍ Toy 6: Pebbles

Denny's 1991, $4-5 each.
Markings: "Denny's® ©1991 H-B Prod Inc Lic by HPI China"

Row 4: Flintstones Vehicles-6 per set:
- ❍ Toy 1: Fred
- ❍ Toy 2: Barney
- ❍ Toy 3: Dino
- ❍ Toy 4: Bamm-Bamm
- ❍ Toy 5: Pebbles
- ❍ Toy 6: Wilma

Denny's 1990, $4-6 each.
Markings: "©1990 H-B Prod Inc Lic by HPI China"

Denny's

Row 1: Jetson Planet Balls-6 per set:
- ○ Toy 1: Jupiter-Judy
- ○ Toy 2: Saturn-George
- ○ Also: Earth-Jane, Moon-Astro, Mars-Elroy, and Neptune-Rosie

Denny's 1992, $3-5 each.
One character is printed on each planet ball with some planet info.
No Markings, Printed: "Denny's® (logo)"

Row 2: Jetson Puzzle Ornaments-6 per set:
- ○ Toy 1: Astro
- ○ Toy 2: Elroy
- ○ Toy 3: Judy
- ○ Toy 4: Rosie
- ○ Toy 5: George
- ○ Toy 6: Jane

Denny's 1992, $4-5 each.

Each came in green and purple. K-Mart also distributed similar puzzles.
Markings: "©1992 Denny's Inc® & ©1992 H-B Prod Inc China"

Row 3: Jetson's Spacecards-6 per set:
- ○ Toy 1: Constellations (cards)
- ○ Toy 2: Astronomers (cards)
- ○ Toy 3: Mission Crews (case)
- ○ Also: Spacecraft, Planets, and Phenomenon

Denny's 1992, $3-5 each.
Each came with several round cards and a round case.
Markings: "©1992 Denny's Inc® & ©H-B Prod Inc Made in China"

Row 4: Spinner:
- ○ Toy 1: Denny's Spinner

Denny's 1993, $3-4 each.
Markings: "Denny's® (logo) ©1993 Denny's Inc Made in China"

Domino's & Discovery Zone & Dunkin' Donuts
Row 1: Noids
❍ Toy 1: Noid Book Mark
❍ Toy 2: 4" Bendable Noid
❍ Toy 3: Noid Mini Disk
❍ Toy 4: 6" Window Noid
Domino's Pizza 1986-1993, $4-5 each.
Markings: "©1986 Domino's Pizza All Rights Reserved"
Row 2: Noid PVCs-7 per set:
❍ Toy 1: Sorcerer Noid
❍ Toy 2: Jack-Hammer Noid
❍ Toy 3: Mad Bomber Noid
❍ Toy 4: Angry Noid on Domino's Pizza Box-2
   pieces
❍ Toy 5: Annoyed Noid
❍ Toy 6: Boxer Noid
❍ Toy 7: Ear-Pulling Noid
Domino's Pizza 1987, $4-5 each.

Markings: "©1987 Domino's Pizza All Rights Reserved"
Row 3: Discovery Zone:
❍ Toy 1: Spinner
❍ Toy 2: Dan Marino Football Player
❍ Toy 3: Hackeysack Ball
Discovery Zone 1994, $2-3 each.
Hackeysack balls also distributed by Showbiz and
Subway.
Markings: "Discovery Zone® (logo)"
Row 4: Munchkins-4 per set:
❍ Toy 1: Beach Munchkin
❍ Toy 2: Skateboard Munchkin
❍ Toy 3: Baseball Munchkin
❍ Also: Lady Munchkin
Dunkin' Donuts 1989, $8-10 each.
Markings: "Dunkin' Donuts Inc Made in China ©1989
Martex Corp All Rights Reserved"

40

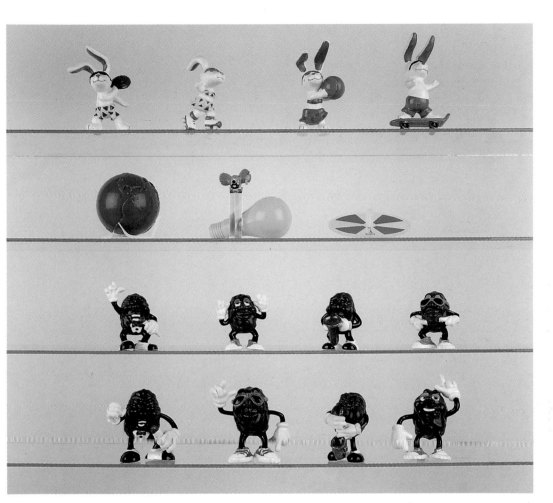

Hardee's

Row 1: Beach Bunnies-4 per set:
○ Toys 1-4 No names
Hardee's 1989, $3-4 each.
Markings: "Beach Bunnies™ ©1989 Applause Inc China"
Row 2: Beakman's World-4 per set:
○ Toy 1: It's a Magnetic World!-3 pieces-inside: horseshoe magnet
○ Toy 2: D'Facts of Light!-3 pieces-inside: prism with Lester the Ratman's head on top
○ Toy 3: Beakman's Whirl!
○ Also: Physics Follies!
Hardee's 1995, $3-4 each.
No Markings
Row 3: California Raisins I-4 per set:
○ Toy 1: Lead Singer with Mike
○ Toy 2: Conga Dancer with Blue Shoes

○ Toy 3: Sax Player
○ Toy 4: Conga Dancer with Orange Glasses
Hardee's 1987, $3-12 each.
A set of these MIP sold for $40 at auction in 1990, placing kid's meal premiums into prominence.
Markings: "©1987 CALRAB Mfg Applause Inc China"
Row 4: California Raisins
○ Toy 1: Lead Singer with Mike
○ Toy 2: Conga Dancer with Orange Glasses
○ Toy 3: Sax Player
○ Toy 4: Conga Dancer with Blue Shoes
Post Raisin Brand 1987, $4-8 each.
These are included to show the size difference. The characters are the same, Hardee's Raisins are more petite.
Markings: "©1987 CALRAB Mfg Applause Inc China"

Hardee's

Row 1: California Raisins II-6 per set:
- ○ Toy 1: Trumpy Trunote
- ○ Toy 2: Captain Toonz
- ○ Toy 3: FF Strings
- ○ Toy 4: Waves Weaver
- ○ Toy 5: SB Stuntz
- ○ Toy 6: Rollin' Rollo

Hardee's 1988, $4-5 each.
Second California Raisin offering.
Markings: "©1988 CALRAB Mfg Applause Inc China"

Row 2: California Raisins IV-4 per set:
- ○ Toy 1: Buster
- ○ Toy 2: Alotta Stile
- ○ Toy 3: Anita Break
- ○ Toy 4: Benny

Hardee's 1991, $4-5 each.
Raisins III is in the Plush & Big section.

Markings: "The Ca Raisins™ ©CALRAB Lic/Mfg by Applause China"

Row 3: Camp California-4 per set:
- ○ Toy 1: Mini Disk
- ○ Toy 2: Bear-squirter
- ○ Toy 3: Mini Volleyball
- ○ Toy 4: Spinner

Hardee's 1993, $2-4 each.
This set is similar to the Camp California set distributed by Carl's Jr.
Markings: "©1992 Camp Cal China"

Row 4: Days of Thunder-4 per set:
- ○ Toy 1: City Chevy #46
- ○ Toy 2: Hardee's #18
- ○ Toy 3: Mello Yello #51
- ○ Toy 4: Superflo #46

Hardee's 1990, $5-7 each.
Markings: "Matchbox® (logo) Matchbox Int'l Ltd ©1990"

Hardee's

Row 1: Dinos
○ Toy 1: Bronto
○ Toy 2: Steggy
○ Also: Rex and Tops
Hardee's 1994, $1-3 each.
Movable with three pieces each.
Markings: "©1994 HFS"
Row 1: Dinosaur in My Pocket-4 per set:
○ Toy 3: Stegosaurus
○ Toy 4: Triceratops
○ Toy 5: Brontosaurus
○ Toy 6: Tyrannosaurus Rex
Hardee's 1993, $1-3 each.
About 2".
Markings: "93 MEG 93 HFS China"
Row 2: Eek! The Cat-3 per set:
○ Toy 1: Eek! The Cat-arms move
○ Toy 2: Annabelle
○ Toy 3: Sharky-squirter
Hardee's 1995, $3-4 each.
Distributed at the same time with The Terrible
Thunderlizards, A TV cartoon series.
Markings: "™ & ©FCN Inc 1995 Hardee's Dakin/China"

Row 3: Eureeka's Castle Stampers-4 per set:
○ Toy 1: Magellan-"Heart" stamp
○ Toy 2: Eureeka-"Star" stamp
○ Toy 3: The Moat Twins-"Circle" stamp
○ Toy 4: Batly-"Square" stamp
Hardee's 1994, $3-4 each.
Stampers.
Markings: "Eureeka's Castle™ on Nick Jr® Made in China
Mfg by Dakin ©1994 Nickeleodeon"
Row 4: Fender Bender 500-5 per set:
○ Toy 1: Yogi & Boo Boo in Jellystone Jammer
○ Toy 2: Huckleberry Hound & Snagglepuss in
    Lucky Trucky
○ Toy 3: Magilla Gorilla & Wally Gator in
    Swamp Stomper
○ Toy 4: Dick Dastardly & Muttley in Dirty
    Truckster
○ Toy 5: Quick Draw McGraw & Baba Looey in
    Texas Twister
Hardee's 1990, $5-6 each.
TV cartoon series by Hanna-Barbera, also distributed by
Carl's Jr.
Markings: "©1990 H-B Prod Inc Lic by HPI China"

Hardee's

Row 1: Flintstones First Thirty Years-5 per set:
- ○ Toy 1: Fred & TV
- ○ Toy 2: Pebbles & Telephone
- ○ Toy 3: Barney & Barbecue
- ○ Toy 4: Bamm-Bamm & Pinball Machine
- ○ Toy 5: Dino & Jukebox

Hardee's 1991, $4-5 each.
TV cartoon series by Hanna-Barbera, two pieces each, about 2" tall.
Markings: "©1991 H-B Prod Inc China"

Row 2: Food Squirters 90-4 per set:
- ○ Toy 1: Hamburger
- ○ Toy 2: Fries
- ○ Toy 3: Strawberry Shake
- ○ Toy 4: Hot Dog

Hardee's 1990, $2-3 each. Toy #4, $4-5.
Water squirters. The hot dog had limited distribution.
Markings: "Hardee's ©1990 Made in China"

Row 2: Food Squirters 93-4 per set:
- ○ Toy 5: Hamburger
- ○ Toy 6: Fries
- ○ Toy 7: Shake
- ○ Also: Hot Dog

Hardee's 1993, $3-4 each. Hot Dog, $4-5.
Fluorescent, same mold as originals. The hot dog had limited distribution.
Markings: "©1990 Made in China Hardee's"

Row 3: Ghostbusters II-4 per set:
- ○ Toy 1: Ghostbuster Siren
- ○ Toy 2: Ghostbuster Siren
- ○ Also: in red and white

Hardee's 1989, $3-5 each.
Recalled. Each has a different electronic sound.
Markings: "Made in Taiwan"

Row 3: Kazoo Crew Sailors-4 per set:
- ○ Toy 3: Captain
- ○ Toy 4: Crewman
- ○ Toy 5: Look-Out
- ○ Toy 6: First Mate

Hardee's 1991, $4-5 each.
Whistles about 5" tall. All have an "H" on them.
Markings: "Lic & Mfg by Applause China"

Hardee's

Row 1: Marvel Comics-4 per set:
- ❍ Toy 1: She-Hulk
- ❍ Toy 2: Mr America
- ❍ Toy 3: Spiderman
- ❍ Toy 4: Hulk

Hardee's 1992, $4-5 each.
Comic book characters. All came with and without the decals on the vehicles.
Markings: "©1990 Marvel Irvine Ca Made in China"

Row 2: Micro Super Soaker-4 per set:
- ❍ Toy 1: Water Cannon
- ❍ Toy 2: Water Gun
- ❍ Toy 3: Bow & Arrow
- ❍ Toy 4: Soak 'n' Fly

Hardee's 1994, $1-2 each.
Squirters.
Markings: "©1994 Larami Corp Lic by LCI Inc ©1994 Hardee's Food Systems Inc Made in China"

Row 3: Muppets Christmas Carol-4 per set:
- ❍ Toy 1: Miss Piggy-as Mrs Kratchet
- ❍ Toy 2: Kermit-as Tiny Tim
- ❍ Toy 3: Gonzo-as Eboneezer Scrooge
- ❍ Toy 4: Fozzie-as Bob Kratchet

Hardee's 1993, $2-3 each.
Finger puppets.
Markings: "©Henson Dakin Made in China"

Row 3: Nicktoons Cruisers-8 per set:
- ❍ Toy 5: Spunky™
- ❍ Toy 6: Tommy Pickles™

Row 4:
- ❍ Toy 1: Ren Hoek™
- ❍ Toy 2: Stimpy™
- ❍ Toy 3: Angelica Pickles™
- ❍ Toy 4: Porkchop™
- ❍ Toy 5: Doug Funnie™
- ❍ Toy 6: Rocko™

Hardee's 1994, $4-5 each.
TV cartoons.
Markings: "©1994 Nickelodeon 1994 Hardee's Dakin/China"

Hardee's

Row 1: Nicktoons Bookmarks-4 per set:
○ Toy 1: Rocko™ & Spunky™
○ Also: Ren & Stimpy, Porkchop & Doug, and Tommy and Angelica
Hardee's 1994, $4-5 each.
Markings: "©1994 Nickelodeon 1994 Hardee's Dakin Mfg by Dakin Inc"
Row 1: Road Runner
○ Toy 2: Road Runner
Hardee's 1993, $4-6.
Markings: "The Ertle Co® Dyersville Iowa USA Made in Taiwan Chevrolet Camero Replica"
Row 1: Smurfs
○ Toys 3-6
Row 2: Smurfs
○ Toys 1-8
Row 3: Smurfs
○ Toys 1-6
Hardee's 1990, $4-6 each.
This is just a sampling of the Smurfs available. Over 100 different Smurfs were given out in Hardee's kid's meals! No list is available. Smurfs were created by Schleich in

Germany and very popular in Europe. Hanna-Barbera made them into the TV cartoon series. All Smurfs are made by Peyo and all are highly collectable. *Markings:* "©Peyo"
Row 3: Christmas Elves:
○ Toys 7 & 8: Christmas Elves
Retail 1978, $4-5 each. These are NOT early Smurfs. Compare the size of their eyes and noses. Christmas Elves are made by Empire and are worthwhile collecting by themselves!
Markings: "(Empire Crown-logo)® Empire ©1978 (Heart-logo) Made in Hong Kong"
Row 4: Smurfs on Skateboards-6 per set:
○ Toy 1: Papa Smurf
○ Toy 2: Swimming Smurf
○ Toy 3: Surfing Smurfette
○ Toy 4: Standing Tall Smurf
·○ Toy 5: Bikini Smurfette
○ Toy 6: Puppy
Hardee's 1990, $4-5 each. Smurfs are named by their activity, these came with a peel-off sticker: "Smurf®"
Markings: "Smurf® ©Peyo Licensed by Applause Licensing China"

Hardee's

Row 1: Snowballs-4 per set:
- ○ Toy 1: Stove Pipe Hat
- ○ Toy 2: Ski Cap & Goggles
- ○ Toy 3: Yankee Cap with Ear Flaps
- ○ Toy 4: Scottish Tam

Hardee's 1994, $2-4 each.
Water squirters, white but change color when wet or cold.
Markings: "Use Ice Water ©1994 Hardee's Food Systems Inc"

Row 2: Speed Bunnies-4 per set:
- ○ Toy 1: Cruiser-Roller Blades
- ○ Toy 2: Dusty-Skateboard
- ○ Toy 3: Sunny-Wind Surfer
- ○ Toy 4: Stretch-Speed Walker

Hardee's 1994, $2-3 each.
Markings: "©1993 HFS China"

Row 3: Swan Princess-5 per set:
- ○ Toy 1: Prince Derek
- ○ Toys 2 & 3: Princess Odette/Swan-skirt flips over (both views shown)
- ○ Toy 4: Jean-Bob-2 pieces
- ○ Toy 5: Puffin-walker
- ○ Toy 6: Rothbart-2 pieces: Rothbart & body mask

Hardee's 1994, $4-5 each.
A cartoon motion picture.
Markings: "©1994 Nest Inc Lic by LCI Inc ©1994 Hardee's Food Systems Inc Made in China"

Row 4: Tang Mouth-4 per set:
- ○ Toy 1: Lance
- ○ Toy 2: Tag
- ○ Toy 3: Flap
- ○ Toy 4: Awesome Annie

Hardee's 1991, $4-6 each.
Markings: "Tang™ ©General Foods Mfg Applause Inc China"
China"

Hardee's

Row 1: Tattoads-4 per set:
○ Toy 1: Toadette
○ Toy 2: Toadinator
○ Toy 3: Toad-Dude
○ Toy 4: Toadster
Hardee's 1995, $1-3 each.
Each came with tattoo stickers for toads or kids.
Markings: "©1994 Hardee's Food Systems Inc Made in China"

Row 2: The Terrible Thunderlizards-3 per set:
○ Toy 1: Squatt
○ Toy 2: Kutter
○ Toy 3: Doc
○ Toy 4: Launcher-1 came with each Thunderlizard
Hardee's 1995, $2-3 each.
Launchers. This set was distributed simultaneously with

Eek! The Cat, TV cartoon series.
Markings: "™ & ©1995 FCN Inc 1995 Hardee's Dakin/China"

Row 3: Treasure Trolls-6 per set:
○ Toys 1-6: No names
Hardee's 1993, $1-2 each. Six different hair colors and four different symbols on their tummies: star, heart, circle, and diamond. Also distributed by Long John Silvers, Roy Rogers, Sonic, and Wal-Mart.
Markings: "China"

Row 4: Where's Waldo-4 per set:
○ Toy 1: Waldo
○ Toy 2: Wenda
○ Toy 3: Wizard
○ Toy 4: Woof
Hardee's 1991, $4-5 each. Straw sliders.
Markings: "©MH 91 China"

Hardee's

Row 1: X-Men-4 per set:
○ Toy 1: Cyclops vs Commando
○ Toy 2: The Blob vs Wolverine
Row 2:
○ Toy 3: Phantasia vs Storm
○ Toy 4: Rogue vs Avalanche
Hardee's 1995, $4-5 each.
Three pieces each. Also distributed by Roy Rogers.
Markings: "™ & ©1995 Marvel 1995 Hardee's Dakin/
China"

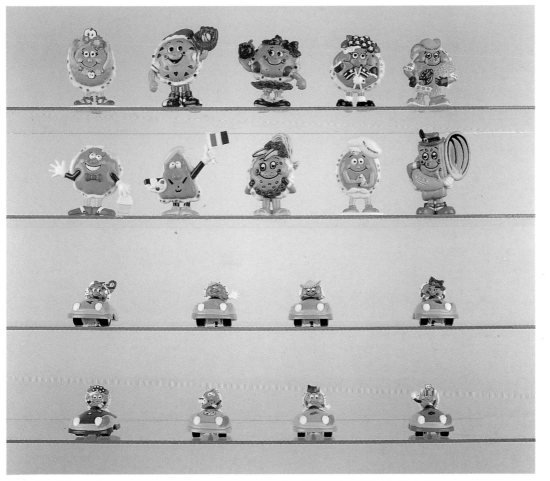

International House of Pancakes

Row 1: Pancake Kids-10 per set:
○ Toy 1: Cynthia Cinnamon Apple
○ Toy 2: Chocolate Chip Charlie
○ Toy 3: Susie Strawberry
○ Toy 4: Bonnie Blueberry
○ Toy 5: Harvey Harvest
Row 2:
○ Toy 6: Betty Buttermilk
○ Toy 7: Frenchy
○ Toy 8: Rosanna Bananna Nut
○ Toy 9: Peter Potato
○ Toy 10: Von der Gus
International House of Pancakes 1992, $4-6 each.
Markings: "IHOP® Restaurant Made in China"

Row 3: Pancake Kid Cruisers-8 per set:
○ Toy 1: Chocolate Chip Charlie
○ Toy 2: Betty Buttermilk
○ Toy 3: Harvey Harvest
○ Toy 4: Susie Strawberry
Row 4:
○ Toy 5: Bonnie Blueberry
○ Toy 6: Frenchy
○ Toy 7: Von der Gus
○ Toy 8: Cynthia Cinnamon Apple
International House of Pancakes 1994, $4-6 each.
There was also a set of three plush Pancake Kids (not
shown).
Markings: "©1993 International House of Pancakes Made
in China"

Jack-in-the-Box

Row 1: Jack Pack Bendable Buddies 91-
5 per set:
- ○ Toy 1: Jumbo Jack
- ○ Toy 2: Sly Fry
- ○ Toy 3: Ollie O Ring
- ○ Toy 4: Edgar E Eggroll
- ○ Toy 5: Betty Burger

Jack-in-the-Box 1991, $8-15 each.
Markings: "Jack-in-the-Box® (logo) Made in China"

Row 2: Jack Pack Bendable Buddies 92-
5 per set:
- ○ Toy 1: Sly Fry
- ○ Also: Jumbo Jack, Ollie O Ring, Betty Burger, and Edgar E Eggroll

Jack-in-the-Box 1992, $8-15 each.
Markings: "Jack-in-the-Box® (logo) Made in China"

Row 3: Jack-in-the-Box People-5 per set:
- ○ Toy 1: Jack

- ○ Toy 2: Spy
- ○ Toy 3: Clown
- ○ Toy 4: German
- ○ Toy 5: O Ring

Jack-in-the-Box 1980s, $15-20 each.
Bendables. Note: these were all found on the east coast-they travel!
Markings: "Jack-in-the-Box® Imperial (Crown-logo) Hong Kong"

Row 4: Jack Pack Finger Puppets-5 per set:
- ○ Toy 1: Jumbo Jack
- ○ Toy 2: Sly Fry
- ○ Toy 3: Ollie O Ring
- ○ Toy 4: Edgar E Eggroll
- ○ Toy 5: Betty Burger

Jack-in-the-Box 1993, $6-10 each.
Finger puppets.
Markings: "Jack-in-the-Box® (logo) Made in China"

K-Mart & Kentucky Fried Chicken & Lee's Famous Recipe Country Chicken

Row 1: Cosmic Flyers-3 per set:
○ Toys 1-3 Cosmic Flyers
K-Mart 1994, $4-5 each.
Glows-in-the-Dark! 7" diameter.
Markings: "Humphery Flyer Made in USA" Label: ©1994 K-Mart Corp"
Row 2: Leaky Tiki Totems-3 per set:
○ Toy 1: Loony Lagoony
○ Toy 2: Golly Wally
○ Toy 3: Silly Spilly
K-Mart 1994, $5-7 each.
Squirters. They can stack on top of each other. Each squirter came with a sheet of 4 different peel-off face stickers.
Markings: "©1994 Peterson-Kennedy All Rights Reserved ©1994 K-Mart Corp China"
Row 2: Puzzle Ornaments-3 per set:
○ Toy 4: Diamond Puzzle
○ Toy 5: Square Puzzle
○ Also: Round Puzzle

K-Mart 1994, $4-6 each.
Similar puzzles were distributed by Denny's.
Markings: "Kid's SM Meals"
Row 3: Kentucky Fried Chicken
○ Toy 1: KFC Flyer
○ Toy 2: KFC Truck
Kentucky Fried Chicken , $4-5 each.
Mini-disk has a 4" diameter.
Markings: "Humphrey Flyer Made in USA" and "yatming Made in Thailand" Truck decals: "KFC® Colonel's Kids"
Row 3: Cartoon Parade-5 per set:
○ Toy 3: Mighty Mouse Viewer
○ Toy 4: Porky Pig Viewer
○ Toy 5: Bugs Bunny Viewer-paper label missing
○ Also: Popeye Viewer and Woody Wood-pecker Viewer
Lee's Famous Recipe Country Chicken 1993, $8-12 each.
Mini-viewers with cartoon strips.
Markings: "Hong Kong" Printed Decal: "Lee's Famous Recipe Country Chicken"

Little Caesar & Long John Silver's
Row 1: Little Caesar-4 per set:
○ Toy 1: Little Caesar Squirter
○ Toy 2: Little Caesar Spinner
○ Toy 3: Little Caesar Ball
○ Toy 4: Little Caesar Popper
Little Caesar's Pizza, $2-4.
No Markings
Row 2: Little Caesar Caesar
○ Toy 1: Roll Em! Roll Em!
○ Toy 2: Blimp! Blimp!
○ Toy 3: Scuba! Scuba!
○ Toy 4: Pepperoni Flyer
○ Toy 5: Knock Down
○ Toy 6: Pan Pipes
○ Toy 7: Secret Ring
Little Caesar's Pizza 1992-5, $2-4 each.
Markings: "©1992 LCE Inc China"
Row 3: Fish Cards

○ Toy 1: Fish Cards
Long John Silver's 1989, $4-6.
"Go Fish" card game.
Printed: "©1989 Long John Silver's All Rights Reserved"
Row 3: Go Fish Cars
○ Toys 2-4: Fish-Cars
Long John Silver's 1986, $8-12 each.
Peel-off stickers for details, various colors and stickers.
Markings: "Not intended for children under three"
Row 4: Once Upon a Forest-5 per set:
○ Toy 1: Abigail
○ Toy 2: Cornelius
○ Toy 3: Edgar
○ Toy 4: Michelle
○ Toy 5 & 6: Russell-2 different mold colors
Long John Silver's 1993, $5-8 each.
Straw Sliders, a cartoon motion picture.
Markings: "™ & ©1993 TCFFC"

Long John Silver's
Row 1: Sea Walkers-5 per set:
○ Toy 1: Tommy
○ Toy 2: Sylvia
○ Toy 3: Sydney
○ Toy 4: Quinn
○ Toy 5: Captain Flint
Long John Silver's 1990, $5-6 each.
Each walker has a name disk to pull the critter into a walk.
No Markings
Row 2: Sea Watchers-3 per set:
○ Toy 1: Pirates & Parrot-square prism
○ Toy 2: Ship & Fish-linear prism
○ Toy 3: Dolphin & Gator-radial prism
Long John Silver's 1990, $5-6 each.
Prism scopes.
Markings: "Long John Silver's Seafood Shoppes"
Row 2: Stone Protectors-7 per set:
○ Toy 4: Angus the Soldier-white stone
○ Toy 5: Clifford the Rock Climber-blue stone
○ Toy 6: Cornelius the Samurai-green stone
○ Toy 7: Chester the Wrestler-red stone

○ Toy 8: Zok the Evil Leader-purple stone
○ Toy 9: Zink the Horrible Hatchetman-pink
        stone
○ Also: Maxwell the Accelerator
Long John Silver's 1994, $5-6 each.
About 1.5" tall, each with a different color stone. New Comic book characters.
Markings: "©ACE LDC China"
Row 3: Treasure Trolls-6 per set:
○ Toys 1-6: No names
Long John Silver's 1993, $2-3 each.
Different colors of hair. Also distributed by Hardee's, Roy Rogers, Sonic, and Wal-Mart.
Markings: "China"
Row 4: Water Blasters-4 per set:
○ Toy 1: Long John Silver
○ Toy 2: Captain Flint
○ Toy 3: Billy Bones
○ Also: Ophelia Octopus
Long John Silver's 1990, $4-6 each.
Squirters.
Markings: "Copyright Long John Silver's Inc 1990 Made in China"

McDonald's

Row 1: 101 Dalmations-4 per set:
- ○ Toy 1: Cruella Deville
- ○ Toy 2: Lucky
- ○ Toy 3: Pongo
- ○ Toy 4: The Colonel & Sargent Tibbs

McDonald's 1992, $2-3 each.
A Disney cartoon motion picture.
Markings: "©Disney China"

Row 2: Alvin & The Chipmunks-4 per set & U-3:
- ○ Toy 1: Alvin with Guitar
- ○ Toy 2: Brittney with Jukebox
- ○ Toy 3: Simon with Movie Camera
- ○ Toy 4: Theodore with Rap Machine
- ○ Toy 5: U-3 Alvin at Jukebox

McDonald's 1990, $5-7 each.

Limited distribution, a TV cartoon series.
Markings: "® ©1990 Bagdasarian Prod China The Chipmunk®"

Rows 3 & 4: Animaniacs-8 per set & U-3:
- ○ Toy 1: Bicycle Built for Trio-also U-3
- ○ Toy 2: Dot's Ice Cream Wagon
- ○ Toy 3: Upside-down Yakko
- ○ Toy 4: Yakko Riding Ralph
- ○ Toy 5: Goodskate Goodfeathers
- ○ Toy 6: Slappy & Skippy's Chopper
- ○ Toy 7: Pinky & The Brain Mobile
- ○ Toy 8: Mindy & Buttons' Wild Ride

McDonald's 1994, $2-3 each.
A Warner Brothers cartoon series.
Markings: "™ & ©Warner Brothers China"

McDonald's

Row 1: Astrosniks 83-8 per set:
○ Toy 1: Skater
○ Toy 2: Sport
○ Toy 3: Scout with Flag
○ Toy 4: Robo
○ Toy 5: Thirsty
○ Toy 6: Laser
○ Toy 7: Astralia with Ice Cream Cone
○ Toy 8: Snikapotamus
McDonald's 1983, $4-8 each.
Limited distribution, all with the arches logo, from a TV cartoon series.
Markings: "©83 Bully-Figuren™ Astrosnik McDonald's® Hong Kong"
Row 2: Astrosniks 84-6 per set:
○ Toy 1: Racing Sled
○ Toy 2: Drill
○ Toy 3: Perfido Man
○ Toy 4: Commander
○ Toy 5: Copter-Rotobackpack
○ Toy 6: Skiing
McDonald's 1984, $4-8 eacn.
Limited distribution, all with the arches logo.

Markings: "©84 Bully-Figuren™ Astrosnik® McDonald's Hong Kong"
Row 3: Astrosniks 85-11 per set:
○ Toy 1: Pyramido
○ Toy 2: Perfido Man
○ Toy 3: Boy with Ice Cream Cone
○ Toy 4: Astrosnik on Rocket
○ Toy 5: Scout
○ Toy 6: Astrosnik with Headphones
○ Also: Laser, Commander, Snikapotamus, Robo, and Astralia
McDonald's 1985, $4-8 each.
Limited distribution, no arches logo on these.
Markings: "©83 Bully-Figuren ©Schaper Astrosniks™ Hong Kong"
Row 4: Attack Pack-4 per set:
○ Toy 1: Truck
○ Toy 2: Battle Bird
○ Toy 3: Sea Creature
○ Toy 4: Lunar Invader
McDonald's 1995, $1-3 each.
Markings: "Attack Pack (logo) Hot Wheels® ©1994 Mattel Inc China Chine"

McDonald's

Row 1: Back to the Future-4 per set:

○ Toy 1: Einstein's Traveling Train
○ Toy 2: Marty's Hoverboard
○ Toy 3: Vern's Junkmobile
○ Toy 4: Doc's Delorean-recalled

McDonald's 1992, $1-3 each. A motion picture.

Markings: "Back to the Future® ©1991 UCS & Amblin ©1991 McDonald's Corp China"

Row 2: Bambi-4 per set & 3 U-3s:

○ Toy 1: Owl
○ Toy 2: Bambi
○ Toy 3: Thumper
○ Toy 4: Flower

Row 3:

○ Toy 5: U-3 Bambi without Butterfly
○ Toy 6: U-3 Thumper
○ Toy 7: U-3 Bambi with Butterfly

McDonald's 1988, $2-5 each; U-3s, $5-7 each.
U-3s have no motion. A Disney cartoon motion picture.

Markings: "©Disney China"

McDonald's

Row 1: Barbie 91
- ○ Toy 1: Hawaiian Fun
- ○ Toy 2: Happy Birthday
- ○ Toy 3: Ice Capades
- ○ Toy 4: Prom
- ○ Toy 5: My First Barbie
- ○ Toy 6: Costume Ball
- ○ Toy 7: Wedding Day Midge
- ○ Toy 8: All American

McDonald's 1991, $4-5 each.
Markings: "Made for McDonald's ©Mattel Inc Made in China"

Row 2: Barbie 92-8 per set:
- ○ Toy 1: My First Ballerina
- ○ Toy 2: Sparkle Eyes
- ○ Toy 3: Rappin' & Rockin'
- ○ Toy 4: Birthday Surprise
- ○ Toy 5: Sun Sensation
- ○ Toy 6: Snap 'N Play
- ○ Toy 7: Rollerblade
- ○ Toy 8: Rose Bride

McDonald's 1992, $4-5 each.
Markings: "Made for McDonald's ©1992 Mattel Inc Made in China"

Row 3: Barbie 93-8 per set & U-3:
- ○ Toy 1: My First Ballerina
- ○ Toy 2: Secret Hearts
- ○ Toy 3: Twinkle Lights
- ○ Toy 4: Hollywood Hair
- ○ Toy 5: U-3 Ball
- ○ Toy 6: Western Stampin'
- ○ Toy 7: Birthday Party
- ○ Toy 8: Romantic Bride
- ○ Toy 9: Paint 'n Dazzle

McDonald's 1993, $3-4 each; U-3, $4-5
Markings: "Made for McDonald's ©Mattel Inc China"

McDonald's

Row 1: Barbie 94-8 per set & U-3:
- ○ Toy 1: Bicyclin'
- ○ Toy 2: Jewel & Glitter Shani
- ○ Toy 3: Camp Barbie
- ○ Toy 4: Camp Teresa
- ○ Toy 5: U-3 Ball
- ○ Toy 6: Locket Surprise-also African-American
- ○ Toy 7: Locket Surprise Ken-also English
- ○ Toy 8: Jewel & Glitter Bride
- ○ Toy 9: Bridesmaid Skipper

McDonald's 1994, $3-4 each; #5 & 6 African-Americans, $5-7 each.
Markings: "Made for McDonald's ©Mattel Inc China"

Row 2: Basic 4-4 per set & U-3:
- ○ Toy 1: Slugger
- ○ Toy 2: Otis
- ○ Toy 3: Milly
- ○ Toy 4: Ruby
- ○ Toy 5: U-3 Dunkan

McDonald's 1993, $1-3 each.
Markings: "©1993 McDonald's Corp China"

Row 3: Batman-4 per set & 1:
- ○ Toy 1: Batmobile
- ○ Toy 2: Catwoman in Cat Coupe
- ○ Toy 3: Penguine in Umbrella
- ○ Toy 4: Batman Press & Go Car
- ○ Toy 5: Batman Returns Minidisk-drink cover

McDonald's 1992, $2-4 each.
A motion picture.
Markings: "©1991 DC Comics China"

McDonald's

Row 1: Batman the Animated Series-
8 per set & U-3:
○ Toy 1: Batman with Removable Cape
○ Toy 2: Batgirl
○ Toy 3: Catwoman & Leopard
○ Toy 4: The Riddler
○ Toy 5: Poison Ivy
○ Toy 6: Robin
○ Toy 7: Two-Face
○ Toy 8: The Joker
○ Also: U-3 Batman with Attached Cape
McDonald's 1993, $2-4 each.
A TV cartoon series.
Markings: "©1993 DC China"
Row 2: Behind the Scenes-4 per set:
○ Toy 1: Animation Wheel
○ Toy 2: Balance Builders-multipieces
○ Toy 3: Rub & Draw Templates
○ Toy 4: Rainbow Viewer
McDonald's 1992, $1-2 each.

Balance builders also distributed by Dairy Queen.
Markings: "©1992 McDonald's Corp China"
Row 3: Berenstain Bears-4 per set & 2 U-3s:
○ Toy 1: Papa & Wheelbarrow
○ Toy 2: Mama & Cart
○ Toy 3: Brother & Scooter
○ Toy 4: Sister & Wagon
○ Toy 5: U-3 Papa-no flocking
○ Toy 6: U-3 Mama-no flocking
McDonald's 1987, $3-5 each; U-3's, $5-7 each.
Markings: "©1986 S&J Berenstain China"
Row 4: Big Foot-4 per set:
○ Toy 1: Ford Pickup
○ Toy 2: Ford Bronco
○ Toy 3: Shuttle Ford
○ Toy 4: MS Ford Pickup
McDonald's 1987, $4-5 each.
Each of the four models came in different colors, with &
without the arches logo, making a total of sixteen
different cars.
Markings: "Bigfoot China"

McDonald's

Row 1: Bobby's World-4 per set & U-3:
- ○ Toy 1: Innertube/Submarine
- ○ Toy 2: Wagon/Race Car
- ○ Toy 3: Skates/Roller Coaster

Row 2:
- ○ Toy 4: 3 Wheeler/Spaceship
- ○ Toy 5: U-3 Innertube-squirter

McDonald's 1994, $1-3 each; U-3, $3-4 A TV cartoon series.

Markings: "©/™ FCN 94 China"

Row 3: Cabbage Patch 92-5 per set & U-3:
- ○ Toy 1: All Dressed Up
- ○ Toy 2: Fun on Ice
- ○ Toy 3: Tiny Dancer
- ○ Toy 4: Holiday Dreamer
- ○ Toy 5: Holiday Pageant
- ○ Toy 6: U-3 Ribbons & Bows

McDonald's 1992, $1-3 each; U-3, $5-6.

Markings: "©1992 OAA China"

Row 4: Cabbage Patch 94-4 per set & U-3:
- ○ Toy 1: Abigail Lynn
- ○ Toy 2: Mimi Kristina
- ○ Toy 3: Michelle Elyse
- ○ Toy 4: Kimberly Katherine
- ○ Toy 5: U-3 Sarajane

McDonald's 1994, $1-3 each; U-3, $4-5.

Markings: "©1994 OAA Inc China"

McDonald's

Row 1: Chip 'n Dale: Rescue Rangers.
4 per set & 2 U-3s:
○ Toy 1: Chip's Whirley-Copter
○ Toy 2: Dale's Roto Roadster
○ Toy 3: Gadget's Rescue Racer
○ Toy 4: Monteray Jack's Propel-A-Phone
○ Toy 5: U-3 Gadget in Rockin' Rider
○ Toy 6: U-3 Chip in Rockin' Racer
McDonald's 1990, $3-4 each.
Disney TV cartoon series.
Markings: "©Disney China RR (logo)"
Row 2: Dink the Little Dinosaur-6 per set:
○ Toy 1: Flapper
○ Toy 2: Shyler
○ Toy 3: Dink
○ Toy 4: Amber
○ Toy 5: Crusty
○ Toy 6: Scat-solid PVC
McDonald's 1990, $5-8 each.
Limited distribution, finger puppets.
Markings: "©1989 Ruby-Spears Inc China"
Row 3: Dinosaurs-6 per set & U-3:
○ Toy 1: Grandma Ethyl
○ Toy 2: Baby Sinclair
○ Toy 3: Fran Sinclair-2 pieces

○ Toy 4: Earl Sinclair
○ Toy 5: Charlene Sinclair
○ Toy 6: Robbie Sinclair
○ Toy 7: U-3 Baby
McDonald's 1993, $2-3 each; U-3, $2-3.
A Disney TV series.
Markings: "©Disney China"
Row 4: Drive Thru Crew-4 per set:
○ Toy 1: McNugget Speedster
○ Toy 2: Milk Carton Zoomer
○ Also: Egg Roadster and Hamburger Ketchup
　　　　Racer
McDonald's 1990, $5-6 each.
Limited distribution.
Markings: "©1989 McDonald's Corp China"
Row 4: Ducktales 87-4 per set & U-3:
○ Toy 3: Spy Glass
○ Toy 4: Magnifying Glass
○ Toy 5: Watch
○ Toy 6: Quaker Whistle-also sold retail
○ Also: U-3 Magic Motion Map
McDonald's 1987, $3-5 each; U-3, $5-6.
TV cartoon series.
Markings: "©1987 McDonald's Corp Made in W
Germany"

61

McDonald's

Row 1: Disneyland 40th Anniversary Parade-
8 per set & U-3:
- ❍ Toy 1: Simba in The Lion King Celebration
- ❍ Toy 2: Brer Bear on Splash Mountain
- ❍ Toy 3: U-3 Winnie the Pooh on Big Thunder
  Mountain Railroad-also with viewer
- ❍ Toy 4: Aladdin & Jasmine at Aladdin's Oasis

Row 2:
- ❍ Toy 5: Mickey Mouse on Space Mountain
- ❍ Toy 6: Roger Rabbit in Benny in Mickey's
  Toontown
- ❍ Toy 7: King Louie on the Jungle Cruise
- ❍ Toy 8: Peter Pan in Fantasmia

McDonald's 1995, $1-3 each. Viewers.
Markings: "©Disney-Amblin China Chine"

McDonald's

Row 1: Ducktales 88-4 per set & U-3:
- ❍ Toy 1: Webby on Tricycle-2 pieces
- ❍ Toy 2: Scrooge McDuck in Car-2 pieces
- ❍ Toy 3: Huey, Dewey & Louie on Jet Ski
- ❍ Toy 4: Launchpad in His Airplane
- ❍ Toy 5: U-3 Huey

McDonald's 1988, $4-6 each; U-3, $6-7.
Limited distribution.
Markings: "©1987 Disney China"
Row 2: Flintstone Kids-4 per set & U-3:
- ❍ Toy 1: Wilma & Dragon
- ❍ Toy 2: Betty & Pteradactyl
- ❍ Toy 3: Fred & Crocasaurus
- ❍ Toy 4: Barney & Mastodon
- ❍ Toy 5: U-3 Dino

McDonald's 1988, $7-10 each; U-3, $12-20.
Limited distribution, two pieces each (except U-3). TV

cartoon series by Hanna-Barbera.
Markings: "©1988 H-B Prod Inc China"
Row 3: Flintstones-5 per set & U-3:
- ❍ Toy 1: Fred & Bedrock Bow-O-Rama-3
  pieces
- ❍ Toy 2: Barney & Fossil Fill-Up-3 pieces
- ❍ Toy 3: Pebbles, Dino & Toy-S-Aurus-2 pieces
Row 4:
- ❍ Toy 4: Wilma & The Flintstone House-2
  pieces
- ❍ Toy 5: Betty & Bamm-Bamm & Roc Donald's-
  3 pieces
- ❍ Toy 6: U-3 Rocking Dino

McDonald's 1994, $1-2 each; U-3, $3-5 each.
A motion picture, two units each-a building to "garage"
the vehicles. Details are peel-off stickers.
Markings: "©UCS & Amblin China"

McDonald's

Row 1: Fraggle Rock-4 per set & 2 U-3s:
○ Toy 1: Red in Radish Car
○ Toy 2: Wimbly & Goober in Cucumber Car
○ Toy 3: Gobo in Carrot Car
○ Toy 4: Mokey in Eggplant Car
○ Toy 5: U-3 Gobo with Carrot
○ Toy 6: U-3 Red with Radish
McDonald's 1988, $1-3 each; U-3s, $3-4 each.
Jim Henson's Puppet characters TV series.
Markings: "©Henson Associates China"
Row 2: Fry Benders-4 per set & U-3:
○ Toy 1: Grand Slam
○ Toy 2: Freestyle
○ Toy 3: Roadie
○ Toy 4: Froggy
○ Toy 5: U-3 Tunes
McDonald's 1989, $3-5 each; U-3, $5-6.

Three pieces each (except U-3).
Markings: "©1989 McDonald's China"
Row 3: Fun with Food-4 per set:
○ Toy 1: McNugget Guys
○ Toy 2: Hamburger Guy
○ Toy 3: French Fry Guy
○ Toy 4: Soft Drink Cup & Lid Guy
McDonald's 1989, $2-4 each.
Multipieces each.
Markings: "©1988 McDonald's Corporation China"
Row 4: Funny Fry Friends-8 per set & 2 U-3s:
○ Toy 1: Hoops
○ Toy 2: Matey
○ Toy 3: Tracker
○ Toy 4: Sweet Cuddles
○ Toy 5: Rollin' Rocker
(Continued in next photo)

McDonald's

Row 1: Funny Fry Friends-8 per set & 2 U-3s-(continued from previous photo):
- ○ Toy 6: ZZZ's
- ○ Toy 7: Gadzooks
- ○ Toy 8: Too Tall
- ○ Toy 9: U-3 Cowgirl
- ○ Toy 10: U-3 Indian

McDonald's 1989, $4-5 each.
Three pieces each.
Markings: "©1989 McDonald's Corporation China"

Row 2: Garfield-4 per set & 2 U-3s:
- ○ Toy 1: In 4-Wheeler
- ○ Toy 2: On Skateboard
- ○ Toy 3: On Scooter
- ○ Toy 4: On Motorcycle with Odie in Sidecar
- ○ Toy 5: U-3 On Skateboard
- ○ Toy 6: U-3 On Skates

McDonald's 1989, $3-5 each; U-3s, $5-7 each.
Limited distribution.
Markings: "©1988 McDonald's China"

Row 3: Ghostbusters-6 per set:
- ○ Toy 1: Stay Puft Marshmallow Man Pencil Sharpener
- ○ Toy 2: Ghostbusters Eraser

- ○ Toy 3: Slimer Pencil Topper
- ○ Also: Pencil, Pencil case, Notepad, Ruler

McDonald's 1987, $5-6 each.
Markings: "©1984 Columbia Pictures Industries Inc ©1987 Columbia Pictures Television A Division of CPT Holdings"

Row 3: Gravedale High-4 per set & U-3:
- ○ Toy 4: Sid (The Invisible Kid)
- ○ Toy 5: Frankentyke
- ○ Toy 6: Cleofatra-also U-3
- ○ Toy 7: Vinnie Stoker

McDonald's 1990, $5-6 each.
Limited distribution.
Markings: "©1991 NBC Made in China"

Row 4: Halloween McNugget Buddies-6 per set & U-3:
- ○ Toy 1: McNuggula
- ○ Toy 2: McBoo McNugget-also U-3
- ○ Toy 3: Pumpking McNugget
- ○ Toy 4: Monster McNugget
- ○ Toy 5: Mummie McNugget
- ○ Toy 6: Witchie McNugget

McDonald's 1992, $2-4 each.
Markings: "©1992 McDonald's Corp Made in China"

McDonald's

Row 1: Happy Birthday-15 per set:
- ○ Toy 1: Ronald McDonald™
- ○ Toy 2: Barbie™-recalled
- ○ Toy 3: Hot Wheels™
- ○ Toy 4: ET®
- ○ Toy 5: Sonic The Hedgehog™

Row 2:
- ○ Toy 6: The Berenstain Bears™
- ○ Toy 7: Tonka®-two pieces
- ○ Toy 8: Cabbage Patch Kids®
- ○ Toy 9: 101 Dalmatians
- ○ Toy 10: Disney's The Little Mermaid®

Row 3:
- ○ Toy 11: Jim Henson's Muppet Babies™
- ○ Toy 12: Peanuts®

- ○ Toy 13: Tiny Toons®
- ○ Toy 14: Looney Tunes™
- ○ Toy 15: The Happy Meal® Guys

McDonald's 1995 , $2-4 each.
All have motion and hook together.
Markings: "©1994 McDonald's Corp China"

Row 4: Hook-4 per set & U-3:
- ○ Toy 1: Peter Pan-3 pieces
- ○ Toy 2: Rufio Squirter also U 3
- ○ Toy 3: Wind-Up Mermaid
- ○ Toy 4: Hook-2 pieces

McDonald's 1992, $1-3 each.
A motion picture.
Markings: "©1991 Tri-Star Pictures Inc ©1991 McDonald's Corp"

McDonald's

Row 1: Hot Wheels 91-8 per set & U-3:
- ○ Toy 1: '55 Chevy
- ○ Toy 2: '63 Vette
- ○ Toy 3: '57 T-Bird
- ○ Toy 4: Camaro Z28
- ○ Toy 5: '55 Chevy

Row 2:
- ○ Toy 6: '63 Vette
- ○ Toy 7: '57 T-Bird
- ○ Toy 8: Camaro Z28
- ○ Toy 9: U-3 Wrench & Hammer

McDonald's 1991, $2-4 each; U-3, $4-6.
Markings: "Hot Wheels® ©Mattel Inc 1978 Malaysia"

Row 3: Hot Wheels 93-8 per set & U-3:
- ○ Toy 1: McDonald's Funny Car
- ○ Toy 2: Quaker State Racer
- ○ Toy 3: McDonald's Thunderbird
- ○ Toy 4: Hot Wheels Funny Car
- ○ Toy 5: McDonald's Dragster

Row 4:
- ○ Toy 6: Hot Wheels Camaro
- ○ Toy 7: Duracell Racer
- ○ Toy 8: Hot Wheels Dragster
- ○ Toy 9: U-3 Wrench & Hammer

McDonald's 1993, $2-3 each; U-3, $4-6.
Markings: "Hot Wheels ©1993 Mattel Inc"

McDonald's

Row 1: Hot Wheels 94-8 per set & U-3:
○ Toy 1: Bold Eagle
○ Toy 2: Black Cat
○ Toy 3: Flame Rider
○ Toy 4: Gas Hog
○ Toy 5: Turbine 4-2
Row 2:
○ Toy 6: 2-Cool
○ Toy 7: Street Shocker
○ Toy 8: X21J Cruiser
○ Toy 9: U-3 fast Forward Vehicle
 McDonald's 1994, $ 1-3 each; U-3, $4.
Markings: "©1994 Mattel Inc Hot Wheels China"
Row 3: Jungle Book-4 per set & 2 U-3s:
○ Toy 1: Shere Khan
○ Toy 2: Kaa
○ Toy 3: King Louie

○ Toy 4: Baloo
○ Toy 5: U-3 Junior
○ Toy 6: U-3 Mowgli
McDonald's 1989, $2-4 each; U-3s, $6-9 each.
A Disney cartoon motion picture.
Markings: "©Disney China"
Row 4: Kisseyfur-8 per set:
○ Toy 1: Gus the Bear
○ Toy 2: Floyd the Alligator
○ Toy 3: Jolene the Alligator
○ Toy 4: Kisseyfur
○ Toy 5: Lennie the Warthog-flocked
○ Toy 6: Toot the Beaver-flocked
○ Toy 7: Behonie the Rabbit-flocked
○ Toy 8: Duane the Pig-flocked
McDonald's 1987, $5-8 each.
Limited distribution.
Markings: "©1985 Phil Mendez Made in China"

McDonald's

Row 1: Little Mermaid-4 per set:
- ◯ Toy 1: Prince Eric & Sebastian-2 pieces
- ◯ Toy 2: Ariel with Seahorse
- ◯ Toy 3: Flounder Squirter-marked: "©Disney"
- ◯ Toy 4: Ursula the Sea Witch

McDonald's 1989, $3-4 each.
A Disney cartoon motion picture. Little Mermaid toys were also distributed by Burger King.
Markings: "©Disney China"

Row 2: Looney Tunes Quack-Up Cars-
4 per set & U-3:
- ◯ Toy 1: Taz in Tornado Tracker
- ◯ Toy 2: Daffy in Splittin' Sportster
- ◯ Toy 3: Porky in Ghost Catcher
- ◯ Toy 4: Bugs in Super Stretch Limo-also in red
- ◯ Toy 5: U-3 Bugs in Swingin' Sedan-also in orange

McDonald's 1993, $1-3 each; orange, $4-6 each.
With the color change, there is a total of seven collectibles here. The orange Bugs' cars had limited distribution.
Markings: "™ & ©92 Warner Bros China"

Row 3: M Squad-4 per set & U-3:
- ◯ Toy 1: Spynoculars
- ◯ Toy 2: Spycoder
- ◯ Toy 3: Spytracker/Watch/Compass
- ◯ Toy 4: Spy Stamper/Calculator
- ◯ Toy 5: U-3 Watch-no compass

McDonald's 1992, $1-3 each.
Markings: "©1992 McDonald's Corp Made in China"

Row 4: Mac Tonight
- ◯ Toys 1-3 Mac Tonight

McDonald's 1991, $5-8 each.
Some of these figurines were distributed to some customers in the restaurants. Others were sold in retail stores.
Markings: "©1998 McDonald's Corp Button Up Company China"

McDonald's

Row 1: MacTonight-6 per set & U-3:
- ○ Toy 1: Off Roader
- ○ Toy 2: Motorscooter
- ○ Toy 3: Porsche
- ○ Toy 4: Surf Ski-with & without wheels
- ○ Toy 5: Motorcycle
- ○ Toy 6: Airplane-with blue or black glasses
- ○ Toy 7: U-3 Skateboard

McDonald's 1991, $4-6 each; U-3, $5-7.
Limited distribution.
Markings: "©1988 McDonald's China"

Row 2: Magic School Bus-4 per set & U-3:
- ○ Toy 1: Undersea Adventure Game
- ○ Toy 2: In the Solar System
- ○ Toy 3: Collector Card Kit
- ○ Toy 4: Geo-Fossil Finder
- ○ Toy 5: U-3 Undersea Adventure Game

McDonald's 1994, $1-2 each.
PBS TV series.
Markings: "©1994 Scholastic Inc China"

Row 3: Making Movies-4 per set & U-3:
- ○ Toy 1: Sound Effects Machine-also U-3
- ○ Toy 2: Movie Camera
- ○ Toy 3: Director's Megaphone
- ○ Toy 4: Clapboard

McDonald's 1994, $1-2 each.
Markings: "©1993 McDonald's Corp China"

Row 4: McDonald's Airport-6 per set & 2 U-3s:
- ○ Toy 1: Ronald's Seaplane
- ○ Toy 2: Fry Guy Flyer
- ○ Toy 3: Birdie Bent Wing Blazer
- ○ Toy 4: Grimace Ace Biplane

(continued in next photograph)

McDonald's

Row 1: McDonald's Airport-(continued from previous photograph):
- Toy 5: Fry Guy Hello Copter
- Toy 6: Big Mac Helicopter-dated 1982
- Toy 7: U-3 Grimace Smiling Shuttle
- Toy 8: U-3 Fry Guy Friendly Flyer

McDonald's 1986, $4-5 each; U-3, $3-4 each.
Various colors for each.
Markings: "©1986 McDonald's Made in USA"

Row 2: McDonald's Bedtime-1 figurine:
- Toy 1: Ronald

McDonald's 1988, $2-4.
Limited distribution.
Marking: "Ronald McDonald® ©1988 McDonald's Corp Made in China"

Row 2: McDonald's Carnival-4 per set & U-3:

- Toy 2: Ronald on Carousel
- Toy 3: Birdie on Swing

Row 3:
- Toy 4: Hamburgular on Ferris Wheel
- Toy 5: Grimace on Turn-Around
- Toy 6: U-3 Grimace

McDonald's 1990, $3-5 each; U-3, $5-6. Multipieces.
Markings: "©1990 McDonald's China"

Row 4: McDonald's Circus Parade-4 per set:
- Toy 1: Ronald Ringmaster
- Toy 2: Bareback Rider Birdie
- Toy 3: Elephant Trainer Fry Guy
- Toy 4: Grimace Playing Calliope

McDonald's 1989, $5-6 each.
Limited distribution.
Markings: "©1989 McDonald's Corp China"

McDonald's

Row 1: McDonald's Connectibles and Linkables-4 per set:

○ Toy 1: Grimace in Wagon
○ Toy 2: Ronald in Soap Box Racer
○ Toy 3: Birdie on Tricycle
○ Toy 4: Hamburgular in Airplane

McDonald's 1991 & 1993, $3-5 each.
Limited distribution, the same set was given out with different names at different times.
Markings: "©1990 McDonald's Corp China"

Row 2: McDonald's Crazy Vehicles-4 per set:

○ Toy 1: Ronald
○ Toy 2: Grimace
○ Toy 3: Hamburgular
○ Toy 4: Birdie

McDonald's 1990, $4-5 each.
Limited distribution, three pieces each.
Markings: "©1990 McDonald's Corp China"

Row 3: McDonald's Design-O-Saurs-
4 per set & 2 U-3s:

○ Toy 1: Fry Guy on McBronto
○ Toy 2: Hamburgular on McTops
○ Toy 3: U-3 Team McDonald's
○ Toy 4: U-3 Happy Tuxi
○ Also: Grimace on McDactyl and Ronald on McRex

McDonald's 1987, $3-4 each.
Various colors.
Markings: "©1987 McDonald's® Corporation Made in USA"

Row 4: McDonald's Fast Macs-5 per set:

○ Toy 1: Hamburgular
○ Toy 2: Big Mac
○ Toy 3: Ronald
○ Toy 4: Birdie
○ Also: Mayor McCheese in Sun Cruiser

McDonald's 1984, $2-5 each; Mayor McCheese, $5-6.
Markings: "McDonald's Corp ©1984 the Ertle Co® Dyersville Iowa USA Made in Hong Kong"

Row 4: McDonald's Feeling Good-2 figurines:

○ Toy 5: U-3 Grimace in Tub
○ Toy 6: U-3 Fry Guy on Duck

McDonald's 1985, $4-6 each.
Other items are not toys.
Markings: "©1984 ©McDonald's Made in USA"

McDonald's

Row 1: McDonald's Flyers-4 per set:
- ○ Toy 1: Big Mac
- ○ Toy 2: Ronald
- ○ Also: Birdie & Hamburgular

McDonald's 1994, $1-2 each.
Markings: "Safety tested for children 3 and over"

Row 2: McDonald's Friendly Skies-2 per set:
- ○ Toy 1: Ronald-also in white airplane
- ○ Toy 2: Grimace

McDonald's 1992, $6-10 each.
Only distributed on selected United Air Lines Flights.
Markings: "©1991 McDonald's Corp ©1991 United Air Lines Inc China"

Row 2: McDonald's Good Morning-2 per set:
- ○ Toy 1: Clock
- ○ Toy 2: Comb

McDonald's 1990, $2-4 each.
Markings: "©1989 McDonald's Corp China"

Row 3: McDonald's Little Engineer-
5 per set & 2 U-3s
- ○ Toy 1: Ronald

- ○ Toy 2: Fry Guy
- ○ Toy 3: Birdie
- ○ Toy 4: Fry Girl
- ○ Toy 5: Grimace
- ○ Toy 6: U-3 Fry Guy Team McDonald's-also in yellow
- ○ Toy 7: U-3 Grimace in Happy Taxi-also in aqua

McDonald's 1986 #1-4, $4-6 each; #5, $5, #6 & 7, $3-4 each.
Limited distribution, each had peel-off stickers.
Markings: under wheels-Made by Monogram Models

Row 4: McDonald's Movables-6 per set:
- ○ Toy 1: Birdie
- ○ Toy 2: Captain
- ○ Toy 3: Ronald
- ○ Toy 4: Professor
- ○ Toy 5: Hamburgular
- ○ Toy 6: Fry Girl

McDonald's 1988, $4-6 each.
Limited distribution.
Markings: "©1988 McDonald's Corp Made in China"

McDonald's

Row 1: McDonald's Olympic Sports Badges-
6 per set:
❍ Toy 1: Ronald
❍ Toy 2: Birdie
❍ Toy 3: Hamburgular
❍ Toy 4: Grimace
❍ Toy 5: Fry Girl
❍ Toy 6: McCosmo
McDonald's 1988, $4-5 each.
Also distributed in McDonald's Europe.
Markings: "©1988 McDonald's Corp"
Row 2: McDonald's Sailors-4 per set & 2 U-3s:
❍ Toy 1: Ronald-in Airboat (missing boat)
❍ Toy 2: Grimace in Submarine
❍ Toy 3: Hamburgular in Pirate Boat
❍ Toy 4: U-3 Fry Guy on Inner Tube
❍ Also: Fry Kids in Ferry and U-3 Grimace on
   Speed Boat
McDonald's 1987, $4-5 each.
Limited distribution.
Markings: "©1987 McDonald's Corp"

Row 3: McDonald's Turbo Macs-
5 per set & U-3:
❍ Toy 1: Birdie
❍ Toy 2: Ronald
❍ Toy 3: Big Mac
❍ Toy 4: Hamburgular
❍ Toy 5: Grimace
❍ Toy 6: U-3 Ronald
McDonald's 1985, $4-6 each; U-3, $6-7.
Limited distribution in USA, also given out in McDonald's
Canada.
Markings: "McDonald's ©1985 Macau"
Row 4: McDonald's Water Games-
4 per set & U-3:
❍ Toy 1: Birdie
❍ Toy 2: Ronald
❍ Toy 3: Hamburgular
❍ Toy 4: Grimace
❍ Toy 5: U-3 Grimace
McDonald's 1992, $5-7 each.
Limited distribution.
Markings: McDonald's logo

McDonald's

Row 1: McDonald's United Airlines
❍ Toy 1: Building
McDonald's 1994, $6-10
Came with small airplane, peel-off stickers, door opens. Given out on selected United Airlines Flights.
Markings: "©1994 McDonald's Corp ©United Airlines Inc China"
Row 2: McDonaldland Junction-4 per set:
❍ Toy 1: Steam Engine-(Ronald missing)-also in blue
❍ Toy 2: Coach with Birdie-also in pink
❍ Toy 3: Flat Car-(Fry Kids missing)-also in white
❍ Toy 4: Caboose with Grimace-also in purple
McDonald's 1983, $5-7 each.
Limited distribution.
Markings: "©1982 McDonald's Corporation Made in USA"

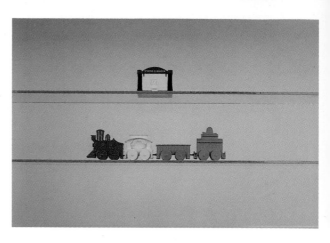

McDonald's

Row 1: McDonaldland (Tricycles)-4 per set:
❍ Toy 1: Ronald
❍ Toy 2: Birdie
❍ Toy 3: Hamburgular
❍ Toy 4: Grimace
McDonald's 1991, $4-5 each.
Limited distribution.
Markings: "©1989 Simon Mkt ©1989 McDonald's Corp"
Row 2: McDonaldland Band-8 per set:
❍ Toy 1: Engine Ronald
❍ Toy 2: Kazoo Birdie
❍ Toy 3: Ronald Pan Pipes
❍ Toy 4: Hamburgular Siren
❍ Toy 5: Fry Girl Trumpet
❍ Toy 6: Fry Guy Boat
❍ Toy 7: Saxophone Grimace
❍ Also: Harmonica
McDonald's 1986, $1 each.

Limited distribution, also sold retail.
Markings: "©1986 McDonald's Corporation Made in USA"
Row 3: McNugget Buddies-10 per set & 2 U-3s:
❍ Toy 1: Mailman
❍ Toy 2: Policeman
❍ Toy 3: Scuba Diver
❍ Toy 4: Drum Major
❍ Toy 5: Popcorn Vender
❍ Toy 6: Tennis Player
Row 4:
❍ Toy 7: Cowpoke
❍ Toy 8: Fireman
❍ Toy 9: Rock Star
❍ Toy 10: Camper
❍ Toy 11: U-3 Daisy
❍ Toy 12: U-3 Slugger
McDonald's 1988, $4-5 each.
Three pieces each.
Markings: "©1988 McDonald's Corp China"

74

McDonald's

Row 1: Mickey & Friends Epcot Center-
8 per set:
- ○ Toy 1: Mickey in USA
- ○ Toy 2: Minnie in Japan
- ○ Toy 3: Daisy in Germany
- ○ Toy 4: Donald in Mexico
- ○ Toy 5: Goofy in Norway
- ○ Toy 6: Dale in Morocco
- ○ Toy 7: Chip in China
- ○ Toy 8: Pluto in France

McDonald's 1994, $3-4 each.
Adventure at Walt Disney World.
Markings: "©Disney China"

Row 2: Mickey's Birthday Land-
5 per set & 4 U-3s:
- ○ Toy 1: Mickey's Roadster
- ○ Toy 2: Minnie's Convertible
- ○ Toy 3: Pluto's Rumbler
- ○ Toy 4: Goofy's Sport Coupe
- ○ Toy 5: Donald's Engine
- ○ Toy 6: U-3 Mickey's Car
- ○ Toy 7: U-3 Minnies' Car
- ○ Toy 8: U-3 Goofy's Car-also in green
- ○ Toy 9: U-3 Donald's Car-also in blue

McDonald's 1988, $2-4 each; U-3s, $6-7 each.

U-3s have a face decal on the hood or roofs (not shown
in picture, sorry).
Markings: "©Disney China"

Row 3: Mighty Mini-4 per set & U-3:
- ○ Toy 1: Pocket Pickup
- ○ Toy 2: Li'l Classic T Bird
- ○ Toy 3: Cargo Climber Van
- ○ Toy 4: Dune Buster
- ○ Toy 5: U-3 Pocket Pickup

McDonald's 1990, $3-4 each.
Limited distribution, Wind-ups.
Markings: "McDonald's Corp China"

Row 4: Mini-Streex-8 per set:
- ○ Toy 1: Black Arrow
- ○ Toy 2: Blade Burner
- ○ Toy 3: Flame Out
- ○ Toy 4: Hot Shock
- ○ Toy 5: Night Shadow
- ○ Toy 6: Quick Flash
- ○ Toy 7: Racer Tracer
- ○ Toy 8: Turbo Flyer

McDonald's 1992, $2-4 each.
The correct launcher is behind each Mini-Streex.
Markings: "©1991 McDonald's Corp Streex is a
Registered Trademark of Mattel Inc Made in China"

McDonald's

Row 1: Mix-Em Up Monsters-4 per set:
- ○ Toy 1: Bibble
- ○ Toy 2: Gropple
- ○ Toy 3: Corkle
- ○ Toy 4: Thugger

McDonald's 1989, $2-4 each.
Also distributed by Avon.
Markings: "Current Inc"

Row 2: Muppet Babies 87-4 per set & 2 U-3s:
- ○ Toy 1: Kermit
- ○ Toy 2: Miss Piggy
- ○ Toy 3: Gonzo
- ○ Toy 4: Fozzie
- ○ Toy 5: U-3 Kermit
- ○ Toy 6: U-3 Miss Piggy

McDonald's 1986, $5-6 each.

Jim Henson's Muppet characters.
Markings: "©1986 McDonald's China"

Row 3: Muppet Babies 90-4 per set:
- ○ Toy 1: Gonzo
- ○ Toy 2: Kermit
- ○ Toy 3: Miss Piggy
- ○ Toy 4: Fozzie

McDonald's 1990, $4-5 each.
Limited distribution.
Markings: "©1990 McDonald's Corp China"

Row 4: Mystery of the Lost Arches-4 per set:
- ○ Toy 1: Phone/Periscope
- ○ Toy 2: Cassette/Magnifier
- ○ Toy 3: Flashlight/Telescope
- ○ Toy 4: Magic Lens Camera-also U-3-recalled

McDonald's 1991, $1 each.
Markings: "©1991 McDonald's Corp China"

McDonald's

Row 1: Muppet Workshop-4 per set:
- ○ Toy 1: Bird
- ○ Toy 2: Dog
- ○ Toy 3: Monster
- ○ Toy 4: What-Not-also U-3

McDonald's 1994, $1 each.
Two removable pieces each, 4" to 6" tall.
Markings: "©Jim Henson Productions Inc China"

Row 2: New Archies-6 per set:
- ○ Toy 1: Archie
- ○ Toy 2: Betty
- ○ Toy 3: Moose
- ○ Toy 4: Jughead
- ○ Toy 5: Veronica
- ○ Toy 6: Reggie

McDonald's 1987, $5-7 each.
Limited distribution.

Markings: "©1987 ACP Made in China ©1988 McDonald's Corp"

Row 3: New Food Changeables to Dinosaurs-8 per set & 2 U-3s:
- ○ Toy 1: Happy-Meal-O-Don
- ○ Toy 2: McDino Cone
- ○ Toy 3: Quarter Pounder Cheese-O-Saur
- ○ Toy 4: McNuggers-O-Saurus
- ○ Toy 5: Mac-O-Saurus Rex

Row 4:
- ○ Toy 6: Tri-Shake-Atops
- ○ Toy 7: Hot-Cakes-O-Dactyl
- ○ Toy 8: Fry-Ceratops
- ○ Toy 9: U-3 Small Fry-Ceratops
- ○ Toy 10: U-3 Bronto Cheeseburger

McDonald's 1991, $3-4 each; U-3s, $4-5 each.
Transformers from food to dinos.
Markings: "©1990 McDonald's Corp"

McDonald's

Row 1: New Food Changeables to Robots-
12-per set & U-3:
- ○ Toy 1: Chicken McNuggets
- ○ Toy 2: Ice Cream Cone
- ○ Toy 3: Shade-circular opening
- ○ Toy 4: Quarter Pounder
- ○ Toy 5: Small White Box Fries
- ○ Toy 6: Cheeseburger
- ○ Toy 7: Big Mac

Row 2:
- ○ Toy 8: Hot Cakes
- ○ Toy 9: Egg McMuffin
- ○ Toy 10: Large Fries-in red box-also blue robot
- ○ Toy 11: Shake-splitting lengthwise
- ○ Toy 12: Quarter Pounder Box
- ○ Toy 13: U-3 Puzzle Cube: Birdie, Hamburgular,
  Grimace, and McCosmo

McDonald's 1987, 1988, $2-3 each; U-3, $5.
Various pieces were distributed with several offers with
several dates.
Markings: "©1987 McDonald's Corporation China"

Row 3: Oliver & Company-4 per set:
- ○ Toy 1: Oliver
- ○ Toy 2: Francis
- ○ Toy 3: Georgette
- ○ Toy 4: Dodger

McDonald's 1988, $2-3 each.
Finger puppets, a Disney cartoon motion picture.
Markings: "©1988 Disney China"

Row 4: Peanuts-4 per set & 2 U-3s:
- ○ Toy 1: Snoopy's Hay Hauler
- ○ Toy 2: Linus' Milk Mover
- ○ Toy 3: Charlie Brown's Seed Bag 'n' Tiller
- ○ Toy 4: Lucy's Apple Cart
- ○ Toy 5: U-3 Snoopy
- ○ Toy 6: U-3 Charlie Brown

McDonald's 1989, $2-4 each; U-3s, $6-8 each.
Three pieces each, except U-3s.
No Markings

McDonald's

Row 1: Piggsbury Pigs-4 per set:
- ○ Toy 1: Portly & Pig Head on Cycle with Side Car
- ○ Toy 2: Rembrant in Barnyard Hot Rod
- ○ Toy 3: Huff & Puff on Catapult-2 pieces
- ○ Toy 4: Piggy & Quackers on Crate Racer

McDonald's 1990, $5-7 each.
Limited distribution.
Markings: "™/©1990 Fox Ch's Net Inc Made in China"

Row 2: Playmobile
- ○ Toy 1: Sheriff
- ○ Toy 2: Indian
- ○ Toy 3: Horse
- ○ Toy 4: Girl-missing Umbrella & Luggage
- ○ Toy 5: Farmer-missing rake

McDonald's 1982, $9-20 each.
The toys were recalled after complaints of small parts.
Under-3 toys were then distributed.
Markings: "©1974 b (logo) Geobra"

Row 3: Polly Pocket-4 per set:
- ○ Toy 1: Bracelet-girls on see-saw
- ○ Toy 2: Watch-gears turn, girls riding the watch hands
- ○ Toy 3: Locket-girl swings
- ○ Toy 4: Ring-petals turn

McDonald's 1995, $1-3.
Markings: "Polly Pocket (logo) ©1994 Blue Bird Toys China Chine"

Row 4: Potato Head Kids-8 per set:
- ○ Toy 1: Slick
- ○ Toy 2: Sabrina
- ○ Toy 3: Spike
- ○ Toy 4: Tulip
- ○ Also: Slugger, Dumpling, Puff, and Spud McDonald's 1992, $3-5 each.

Limited distribution. Also distributed by Avon, Wal-Mart, and Wendy's.
Markings: "©1987 Hasbro Made in China"

McDonald's

Row 1: Raggedy Ann & Andy-4 per set & U-3:
❍ Toy 1: Raggedy Andy with Slide
❍ Toy 2: Raggedy Ann with Swing
Row 2:
❍ Toy 3: The Camel with the Wrinkled Knees & a Seesaw
❍ Toy 4: Grouchy Bear with Carousel
❍ Toy 5: U-3 The Camel
McDonald's 1989, $5-7 each.
Limited distribution.
Markings: "©1988 MacMillian Inc China"
Row 3: Rescuers Down Under-4 per set & U-3:
❍ Toy 1: Jake
❍ Toy 2: Cody
❍ Toy 3: Wilbur
❍ Toy 4: Bernard & Bianca
❍ Toy 5: U-3 Bernard
McDonald's 1990, $2-3 each.
Viewers.

Markings: "©Disney China"
Row 4: Runaway Robots-6 per set:
❍ Toy 1: Beck
❍ Toy 2: Flame
❍ Toy 3: Jab
❍ Toy 4: Bolt
❍ Toy 5: Coil
❍ Toy 6: Skull
McDonald's 1985, $4-5 each.
Limited distribution. Also distributed by Subway (Cy*Treds) and Sonic.
Markings: "©85 S Colburn Made in China"
Row 4: Sea World of Ohio-3 per set:
❍ Toy 7: Shamu
❍ Toy 8: Dolly Dolphin
❍ Also: Penny Penguin
McDonald's 1988, $5-8 each.
Limited distribution.
Markings: "©1987 Sea World Inc Made in China"

McDonald's

Row 1: Snow White-8 per set & U-3:
○ Toy 1: Snow White & Wishing Well
○ Toy 2: Happy & Grumpy
○ Toy 3: Doc
○ Toy 4: Dopey & Sneezy-also U-3
Row 2:
○ Toy 5: Double Trouble Queen/Witch
○ Toy 6: Bashful
○ Toy 7: * Sleepy, $2-4.
○ Toy 8: Prince & Horse-with & without base
McDonald's 1993, $2-4 each; with base, $5-6.
The Prince's Horse came with and without (limited distribution) a grass base.
Markings: "©Disney China"
Row 3: Sonic The Hedgehog 3-4 per set & U-3:

○ Toy 1: Sonic The Hedgehog
○ Toy 2: Miles Tails Prowler-recalled
○ Toy 3: Dr Ivo Robotnik
○ Toy 4: Knuckles
○ Toy 5: U-3 Ball
McDonald's 1994, $1-3 each; U-3, $3-5.
A TV cartoon series and a Sega Video Game.
Markings: "™ & ©1993 Sega China"
Row 4: Sports Balls-4 per set:
○ Toy 1: Basketball
○ Toy 2: Baseball
○ Toys 3 & 4: Football-two colors
○ Toy 5: Soccer Ball
McDonald's 1990, $4-5 each.
Limited distribution.
Tag: "©1989 McDonald's Corporation"

McDonald's

Row 1: Stomper Mini 4x4-8 per set & 4 U-3s:
- ❍ Toy 1: AMC Eagle-also black with gold
- ❍ Toy 2: Chevy S-10 also black with silver
- ❍ Toy 3: Chevy Van-also yellow with orange
- ❍ Toy 4: Chevy Blazer-also yellow with green
- ❍ Toy 5: Dodge Rampage-also white with blue
- ❍ Toy 6: Ford Ranger-also orange with yellow

Row 2:
- ❍ Toy 7: Jeep Renegade-also orange with yellow
- ❍ Toy 8: Toyota Tercel-also blue with yellow
- ❍ Toy 9: U-3 Blazer
- ❍ Toy 10: U-3 Tercel
- ❍ Toy 11: U-3 Chevy Van
- ❍ Toy 12: U-3 Jeep Renegade

McDonald's 1986, $3-5 each. Limited distribution.
Markings: "Stomper® Patent Pending Schaper Mfg Co Minneapolis Mn"

Row 3: Super Heroes-4 per set & U-3:
- ❍ Toy 1: Daffy Duck as Bat-Duck
- ❍ Toy 2: Tazmanian Devil as Taz-Flash
- ❍ Toy 3: Petunia Pig as Wonder Pig
- ❍ Toy 4: Bugs Bunny as Super Bugs
- ❍ Toy 5: U-3 Daffy in Bat-Duckmobile

McDonald's 1992, $2-4 each.
Warner Brothers cartoon characters.
Markings: "™ & ©91 WBI China"

Row 3: Super Mario Brothers-4 per set & U-3:
- ❍ Toy 1: Mario
- ❍ Toy 2: Luigi
- ❍ Toy 3: Goomba
- ❍ Toy 4: Koopa Paratroopa
- ❍ Toy 5: U-3 Mario-finger puppet

McDonald's 1991, $3-5 each.
A video game.
Markings: "©1989 Nintendo of America Inc China"

McDonald's

Row 1: Spiderman-8 per set:
- ❍ Toy 1: Spiderman
- ❍ Toy 2: Mary Jane Watson & 2 Outfits-3 pieces
- ❍ Toy 3: Steve Parker

Row 2:
- ❍ Toy 4: Scorpion Stingstriker
- ❍ Toy 5: Hobgobbin Landglider
- ❍ Toy 6: Venom Transport
- ❍ Toy 7: Spidermobile
- ❍ Also: Dr Octopus

McDonald's 1995, $4-6.
Markings: "©1995 Marvel China Chine"

McDonald's

Row 1: Tailspin-4 per set & 2 U-3s:
- ❍ Toy 1: Wildcat's Flying Machine
- ❍ Toy 2: Baloo's Sea Plane
- ❍ Toy 3: Kit's Racing Plane
- ❍ Toy 4: Molly's Biplane
- ❍ Toy 5: U-3 Baloo
- ❍ Toy 6: U-3 Wildcat

McDonald's 1990, $1-3 each; U-3s, $4-5 each.
A Disney TV cartoon series. Metal airplanes.
Markings: "©Disney China"

Row 2: Tinosaurs-8 per set:
- ❍ Toy 1: Kobby
- ❍ Toy 2: Link
- ❍ Toy 3: Fern
- ❍ Toy 4: Spell
- ❍ Toy 5: Dinah
- ❍ Toy 6: Tiny
- ❍ Toy 7: Jad
- ❍ Toy 8: Bones

McDonald's 1985, $5-8 each. Limited distribution.
Markings: "©85 Aviva Ent Inc Tinosaurs McDonald's® Made in China"

Row 3: Tiny Toons-8 per set & U-3:
- ❍ Toy 1: Buster Bunny
- ❍ Toy 2: Elmyra
- ❍ Toy 3: Dizzy Devil
- ❍ Toy 4: Montana Max
- ❍ Toy 5: Plucky Duck
- ❍ Toy 6: Babs Bunny
- ❍ Toy 7: GoGo DoDo
- ❍ Toy 8: Sweetie-also U-3

McDonald's 1993, $1-3 each.
A Warner Brothers TV cartoon series.
Markings: " ™ & ©Warner China"

Row 4: Tiny Toons Flip Cars-4 per set & 2 U-3s:
- ❍ Toy 1: Montana Max/GoGo DoDo
- ❍ Toy 2: Hampton/Dizzy Devil
- ❍ Toy 3: Elmyra/Buster Bunny
- ❍ Toy 4: Babs Bunny/Plucky Duck
- ❍ Toy 5: U-3 GoGo DoDo
- ❍ Toy 6: U-3 Plucky Duck

McDonald's 1990, $1-3 each; U-3s, $5-10 each.
Markings: "©1990 Warner Brothers ©1990 McDonald's Corp"

McDonald's

Row 1: Tom & Jerry Band-4 per set & U-3:
○ Toy 1: Droopy with Microphone
○ Toy 2: Tom with Keyboard
○ Toy 3: Jerry with Drums
○ Toy 4: Spike with Base
○ Toy 5: U-3 Droopy
McDonald's 1989, $7-9 each.
Limited distribution.
Markings: "©1988 Turner Entertainment Co Made in China"
Row 2: Tonka 92-5 per set & U-3:
○ Toy 1: Backhoe
○ Toy 2: Cement Mixer
○ Toy 3: Fire Truck
○ Toy 4: Loader
○ Toy 5: Dump Truck
○ Toy 6: U-3 Dump Truck

McDonald's 1992, $2-3 each; U-3, $5.
Markings: "©1992 Tonka Corp China"
Row 3: Tonka 94-4 per set & U-3:
○ Toy 1: Loader
○ Toy 2: Grader
○ Toy 3: Crane
○ Toy 4: Bulldozer
○ Toy 5: U-3 Dump Truck
McDonald's 1994, $2-3 each; U-3, $3-5.
Markings: "©1992 Tonka Corp China"
Row 4: Totally Toy Holiday-Boys-4 per set & U-3:
○ Toy 1: Mighty Max
○ Toy 2: Tattoo Machine
○ Toy 3: Key Force Truck
○ Toy 4: Attack Pack
○ Toy 5: U-3 Key Force Car
McDonald's 1993, $2-3 each.
Markings: "Hot Wheels® ©1993 Mattel Inc China"

McDonald's

Row 4: Totally Toy Holiday, Ollie 4 per set.
- ○ Toy 1: Polly Pocket
- ○ Toys 2 & 3: Sally Secrets-shoes are hole
  punch
- ○ Toy 4: Li'l Miss Candy Stripes
- ○ Toys 5 & 6: Magic Nursery-also U-3

McDonald's 1993, $1-3 each.
Markings: "Made for McDonald's ©1993 Bluebird Toys China"

Row 2: Wild Friends-4 per set & U-3:
- ○ Toy 1: Panda
- ○ Toy 2: Alligator
- ○ Toy 3: Elephant
- ○ Toy 4: Gorilla
- ○ Toy 5: U-3 Panda

McDonald's 1992, $5-6 each; U-3, $6-8.
Limited distribution, PVC with book attached to base.
Markings: "©1992 SMI China"

Row 3: Yo, Yogi-4 per set:
- ○ Toy 1: Cindy (Fr-*Cindy*)
- ○ Toy 2: Boo Boo (Fr-*Bou-Bou*)

- ○ Toy 3: Huckleberry Hound (Fr-*Roquet Belles Oreilles*)
- ○ Toy 4: Yogi (Fr-*Yogi*)

McDonald's 1991, $5-8 each.
Limited distribution in USA & distribution in Canada.
Markings: "©1991 H-B Prod Inc China"

Row 4: Young Astronauts 92:
- ○ Toy 1: U-3 Ronald

McDonald's 1992, $3-4 each.
Single figurine, the regular premiums are paper puzzles.
Markings: "©1991 McDonald's Corp Young Astronauts Council™ China"

Row 4: Young Astronauts 94-4 per set & 2 U-3s:
- ○ Toy 2: Apollo Module
- ○ Toy 3: Cirrus VTOL
- ○ Toy 4: Space Shuttle
- ○ Toy 5: U-3 Fry Guy Friendly Flyer
- ○ Toy 6: U-3 Grimace Smiling Shuttle
- ○ Also: Argo Land Shuttle

McDonald's 1986, $8-10 each.
Limited distribution.
Markings: "©1986 McDonald's"

Nathan's

Row 1: Franksters 92-3 per set:
- ○ Toy 1: Rollerblades
- ○ Toy 2: Skateboard
- ○ Toy 3: Ice Skates

Nathan's Famous Hot Dogs 1992, $7-10 each. About 5-6" tall.

Markings: "Since 1916 Nathan's® (logo) ©1992 Nathan's Famous Inc Made in China"

Row 1: Franksters 93-3per set:
- ○ Toy 4: Baseball
- ○ Toy 5: Surfer
- ○ Also: Swimmer

Nathan's Famous Hot Dogs 1993, $7-10 each. About 5-6" tall.

Markings: "Since 1916 Nathan's® (logo) ©1993 Nathan's Famous Inc Made in China"

Row 2: Franksters 94-4 per set:
- ○ Toy 1: Football
- ○ Toy 2: Cheerleader
- ○ Toy 3: Basketball
- ○ Toy 4: Hockey

Nathan's Famous Hot Dogs 1994, $7-10 each. About 5-6" tall.

Markings: "Since 1916 Nathan's® (logo) ©1994 Nathan's Famous Inc Made in China"

Pizza Hut & Popeye's

Row 1: Air Garfield:
○ Toy 1: Air Garfield
Pizza Hut 1993, $1.
This figurine was inside a spaceball or attached to a parachute which is usually how he is found if not MIP.
Markings: "©1978 United Features Syndicate Inc Made in China"

Row 1: Aliens-4 per set:
○ Toy 2: Smiley
○ Toy 3: Little Green Man from Mars
○ Toy 4: Space Kat
○ Toy 5: Moon Man
Pizza Hut 1980s with logo, $12-15 each; no logos, $5-10 each.
These creatures were so popular that they were recast with the markings removed.
Markings: "Pizza Hut (logo) Made in China"

Row 2: Marsupilami Houba-Douba-3 per set:
○ Toy 1: Jump Rope
○ Toy 2: Glow Ball
○ Toy 3: Yo-Yo
Pizza Hut 1994, $4-5 each.
Markings: "©Disney China"

Row 3: Pizza Box
○ Toy 1: Pizza Box
Pizza Hut 1994, $1-2.

Inside of lid has pizza topping food molds, base is pizza crust mold, came with peel-off stickers.
No Markings

Row 3: Young Indiana Jones Chronicles-3 per set:
○ Toy 1: Magnifying Glass
○ Toy 2: Compass
○ Toy 3: Telescope
Pizza Hut 1994, $3-5 each.
A TV series.
Markings: "Don't look into sun China"

Row 4: Popeye-5 per set:
○ Toy 1: Popeye
○ Toy 2: Olive Oyl
○ Toy 3: Sweet Pea
○ Toy 4: Brutus
○ Also: Wimpy
Popeye's Famous Fried Chicken 1980 to 1994, $1-3 each.
About 2" tall each, came in five different colors.
Markings: "1980 KFS"

Row 4: Popeye Pencil Toppers-5 per set:
○ Toy 5: Sweet Pea
○ Also: Olive Oyl, Popeye, Wimpy, and Brutus
Popeye's Famous Fried Chicken 1980 to 1994. $1 each.
About 1.25" tall pencil toppers.
Markings: "©1980 KFS"

Roy Rogers

Rows 1 & 2: Batting Helmets-28 teams per set:
Roy Rogers 1992, $1-2 each.
Markings: "Leich (logo)"
Row 3: Fun Flyers-4 per set:
○ Toy 1: Passenger Plane
○ Toy 2: Helicopter
○ Also: Jet Fighter and Jet Passenger
Roy Rogers 1989, $5-8 each.
Each came in different colors with peel-off stickers.

Markings: "Vikingplast Sweden Art NR"
Row 4: Gator Tales-4 per set:
○ Toy 1: Av Gator
○ Toy 2: Flora Gator
○ Toy 3: Investi-Gator
○ Toy 4: Skater Gator
Roy Rogers 1989, $6-8 each.
Two pieces each: the hair/hats/glasses are easy to lose.
Markings: "Mfg by Procorp Inc Made in China"

Roy Rogers

Row 1: X-Men
○ Toy 1: Cyclops vs Commando
○ Toy 2: The Blob vs Wolverine
Row 2:
○ Toy 1: Phantasia vs Storm
○ Toy 2: Rogue vs Avalanche
Roy Rogers 1995, $4-5 each.
Three pieces each, the four platforms or ground pieces fit together to form one battleground. Also distributed by Hardee's.
Markings: "™ & ©1995 Marvel"

Roy Rogers

Row 1: Skateboard Gang Kids-4 per set.
○ Toys 1-4: No names
Roy Rogers 1989, $5-6 each.
Two pieces each.
Markings: "Mattel Inc 1989 Made in China"
Rows 2 & 3: Snorks:
○ Toys 1-16: Snorks
Names: Leader-"Allstar," Girlfriend-"Casey,"
Friends: "Dimmy" & "Tooter"
Roy Rogers 1988, $4-6 each.
Over thirty different Snorks were given out! Snorks were a

TV cartoon series by Hanna-Barbera, created by Fred
Monnickendam for comic book characters in Belgium
and Europe.
Markings: "©SEPP 1982 Wallace Berrie Schleich Hong
Kong"
Row 4: Treasure Trolls-6 per set:
○ Toys 1-6: Treasure Trolls
Roy Rogers 1993, $1-3 each.
Also distributed by Hardee's, Long John Silvers, Sonic, and
Wal-Mart.
Markings: "China"

Showbiz Pizza

Row 1: Chuck E Cheese-8 per set:

○ Toy 1: Chuck E Cheese
○ Toy 2: Jumpin' Chuck E Cheese
○ Toy 3: Pen Topper
○ Toy 4: Car
○ Toy 5: Van
○ Toy 6: Water Ball
○ Toy 7: Hackeysack Ball
○ Also: Jeep

Showbiz Pizza 1988-1993, $4-6 each.

The whole restaurant is for kids! The prizes are won by collecting tickets from games in the restaurant. New items are added and depleted continually. Hackeysack

balls also distributed by Discovery Zone and Subway.

Markings: "©1988 Showbiz Pizza Time Inc Made in China"

Row 2: Chuck E Cheese Prizes

○ Toy 1: 7" Disk
○ Toy 2: Yo-Yo's
○ Toy 3: Telescope
○ Toy 4: Watch Game

Row 3:

○ Toy 5: Stencils
○ Toy 6: Picture Super Ball
○ Toy 7: Games
○ Toy 8: Color Cup

Showbiz Pizza 1986-1993, $2-5 each.

Markings: "©1986 Showbiz Pizza Time Inc Made in China"

Showbiz Pizza

Row 1: Chuck E Cheese Prizes:
- Toys 1-4: Fluorescent Chucky
- Toy 5: Parachute Chucky
- Toy 6: Mini Disks-3.5" diameter
- Toy 7: Blue Ribbon

Row 2:
- Toy 8: Coin Holder for Quarters/Tokens
- Toy 9: Comb
- Toy 10: Purse
- Toy 11: Pencil Case-encased water & glitter
- Toy 12: Viewer

Showbiz Pizza 1986-1994, $1-3 each.
Markings: "©1988 Showbiz Pizza Time Inc Made in China"
Row 3: Chuck E Cheese Sports-3 per set:
- Toy 1: Basketball
- Toy 2: Baseball
- Toy 3: Football

Showbiz Pizza 1990-1994, $4-6 each.
Markings: "Made in Hong Kong Showbiz Pizza Time Inc™"
Row 3: Pizza Time Theater-2 per set:
- Toy 4: Munch
- Toy 5: Jasper

Showbiz Pizza 1983-1993, $4-6 each.
Pizza Time Theater, Showbiz Pizza, and Chuck E Cheese refer to the same restaurant.
Markings: "©1983 Pizza Time Theater Made in Hong Kong"
Row 3: Pizza Time Theater-2 per set:
- Toy 6: Chuck E Cheese
- Toy 7: Helen

Showbiz Pizza 1994, $3-5 each.
These are the new images; the other PVCs are not longer available from the restaurants.
Markings: "©Showbiz Pizza Time Inc 1994 DFI China"

Sonic

Row 1: Adventures of the Super Sonic Kids-
4 per set:
○ Toy 1: Steve
○ Also: Brin, Corkey, and Rick
Sonic 1989, $4-6 each.
Markings: "China"
Printed: "Sonic" on shirt back
Row 1: Airtoads-6 per set:
○ Toys 2-7: Airtoads-no names
Sonic 1995, $4-5 each.
On suction cups.
No Markings, Printed: "Sonic® Airtoads"
Row 2: Animal Squirters-8 per set:
○ Toy 1: Bear
○ Toy 2: Rabbit
○ Toy 3: Panda
○ Toy 4: Monkey
○ Toy 5: Hound Dog
○ Toy 6: Cat

Row 3:
○ Toy 1: Puppy
○ Toy 2: Bulldog
Sonic 1995, $2-3 each.
Ball squirters.
No Markings
Row 3: Bag-A-Wag-4 per set:
○ Toy 3: Car
○ Toy 4: Walking
○ Toy 5: Skating
○ Toy 6: Resting
Sonic 1992, $3-5 each.
Markings: "©Sonic Ind 1992 Made in China"
Row 4: Brown Bag Bowlers-4 per set:
○ Toy 1: Yellow Ball
○ Toy 2: Red Ball
○ Toy 3: Blue Ball
○ Toy 4: Orange Ball
Sonic 1994, $3-3 each.
Markings: "©1994 Sonic Industries China"

Sonic

Row 1: Brown Bag Juniors-4 per set:
○ Toy 1: Marbles
○ Toy 2: Basketball
○ Toy 3: Reading
○ Toy 4: "The Fonz"
Sonic 1989, $4-5 each.
Markings: "©Sonic Ind Made in China"
Row 2: Brown Bag Sports Buddies-4 per set:
○ Toy 1: Innertube Float
○ Toy 2: Surfboard
○ Toy 3: Sled
○ Toy 4: Skiing
Sonic 1993, $3-5 each.
Markings: "©Sonic Ind 1993 Made in China"
Row 2: Custom Cruisers-4 per set:
○ Toy 5: '59 Cadillac Convertible
○ Also: '49 Mercury, '55 Chevy Nomad Wagon,

and '57 Chevy Convertible
Sonic 1993, $4-6 each.
Markings: "©1993 Sonic Inc China"
Row 3: Dino Hops-4 per set:
○ Toy 1: Dino with Drink
○ Toy 2: Dino with Hamburger
○ Toy 3: Dino with Hot Dog
○ Toy 4: Dino with Fries
Sonic 1994, $3-4 each.
On Springs.
Markings: "©Sonic Inc 1994 China"
Row 4: Dino Squirters-4 per set:
○ Toys 1-4: No names
Sonic 1994, $2-3 each.
Squirters.
Markings: "Sonic® (logo) ©Sonic Ind Inc 1994 ©NPI 1991"

Sonic

Row 1: Flying Food-4 per set:
- ○ Toy 1: Onion Ring Squadron
- ○ Toy 2: Melvin Mini Burger
- ○ Toy 3: Clyde Corn Dog
- ○ Toy 4: Taterites

Sonic 1994, $2-3 each.
Suction disks.
No Markings, Label: "©1994 Sonic Industries Inc Made in China"

Row 2: Glass Hangers-9 per set:
- ○ Toy 1: Frog
- ○ Toy 2: Lion
- ○ Toy 3: Turtle
- ○ Toy 4: Pig
- ○ Toy 5: Elephant
- ○ Toy 6: Beaver
- ○ Toy 7: Gator
- ○ Toy 8: Bear
- ○ Toy 9: Bird

Sonic 1993, $1-2 each.
Various colors each, to hang on the rim of a glass or vase. Also distributed by Wendy's.
No Markings

Row 3: Hair Dudes-4 per set:
- ○ Toys 1-4 No names

Sonic 1993, $3-4 each.
This critter came with grass seeds to grow "hair."
Markings: "©1993 Peterson-Kennedy All Rights Reserved China"

Row 4: Holiday Express-4 per set:
- ○ Toy 1: Engine
- ○ Toy 2: Hopper
- ○ Toy 3: Gondola
- ○ Toy 4: Caboose

Sonic 1993, $5-8 each.
Similar to trains distributed by Dairy Queen and White Castle.
Markings: "Made in China"
Decals: "Sonic" and "Dr Pepper"

Row 1: Sidewalk Surfers 4 per set:
◯ Toy 1: Mr Big Fun
◯ Toy 2: Ms Sidewalk Savvy
◯ Toy 3: The Mean Sidewalk Machine
◯ Toy 4: The Sidewalk Snoot
Sonic 1989, $3-4 each.
Photo does not show cute faces (sorry).
Markings: "Sonic® (logo) Sidewalk Surfers! Made in China
Sonic Industries Inc 1989"
Row 2: Sonic Fast Food Squirters-4 per set:
◯ Toy 1: Hamburger
◯ Toy 2: Fries
◯ Toy 3: Drink
◯ Toy 4: Peppermint

Sonic 1993, $3-4 each.
Water squirters.
Markings: "©1993 Sonic China"
Row 3: Sonic Kid Squirters-3 per set:
◯ Toys 1-3: No names
Sonic 1993, $2-4 each.
Water squirters.
Markings: "Sonic® (logo) ©Sonic Ind Inc 1993
©Namkung 1993 China"
Row 4: Super Sonic Turbo Racers-4 per set:
◯ Toys 1-4: no names
Sonic 1993, $3-5 each.
Fluorescent.
No Markings, Sticker: "Made in China"

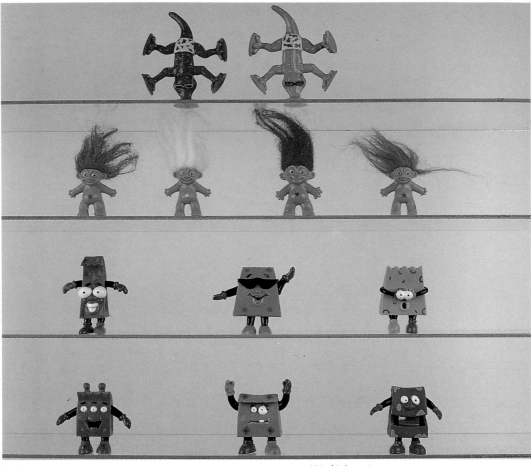

Sonic

Row 1: Stunt Grip Geckos-4 per set:
○ Toy 1: Turquoise
○ Toy 2: Purple
○ Also: Green and Blue
Sonic 1992, $2-4 each.
Same gecko with suction cups on feet.
No Markings
Row 2: Treasure Trolls-4 per set:
○ Toys 1-4: Treasure Trolls

Sonic 1993, $1-2 each.
Also distributed by Hardee's, Long John Silvers, Roy Rogers, and Wal-Mart.
Markings: "China"
Rows 3 & 4: Wacky Sackers-6 per set:
○ Toys 1-6 Wacky Sackers-No names
Sonic 1994, $2-4 each.
Four colors each: pink, blue, green, and tan-twenty-four total.
Markings: "©1994 Sonic Industries China"

Subway

Row 1: Captain Planet 5 per set:

○ Toy 1: Earth (Quami's Ring)
○ Toy 2: Wind (Linka's Ring)
○ Toy 3: Fire (Wheeler's Ring)
○ Toy 4: Water (Gee's Ring)
○ Toy 5: Heart (Mati's Ring)
Subway 1993, $4-6 each.
Heat the blue circle with your finger to see the symbol.
These rings are essential to the characters. A TV cartoon
series. About 1.5" diameter.
Markings: "Subway® Made in USA ©1993 TBS & DIC UGI"

Row 2: Coneheads Pencil Toppers-4 per set:

○ Toy 1: Beldar
○ Toy 2: Marlax
○ Toy 3: Prymaat
○ Also: Connie
Subway 1993, $4-6 each.
A motion picture. About 2.25" tall.
Markings: "©1993 Paramount Pictures Made in China"

Row 3: Cy*Treds-6 per set:

○ Toy 1: Beck
○ Toy 2: Flame
○ Toy 3: Jab

○ Toy 4: Bolt
○ Toy 5: Coil
○ Toy 6: Skull
Subway 1995, $3-4 each.
Also distributed by McDonald's ("Runaway Robots"-note
different markings).
Markings: "Subway® JGI & DAI China"

Row 4: Doodletop Jr-4 per set:

○ Toys: 1-4
Subway 1994, $1-2 each.
Spinning top markers about 2" diameter.
Markings: "Doodletop Jr Pat Pend Made in USA"

Row 4: Hackeysack Balls-5 per set:

○ Toy 5: Tilly Tomato
○ Toy 6: Pearl Onion
○ Also: Pappy Pepper, Petey Pickle, and Lenny
Lettuce
Subway 1991, $2-3 each.
Reverse side shows picture of "vegetable people."
Hackeysack balls also distributed by Discovery Zone and
Showbiz Pizza.
Label: "Subway (logo) Made in China ©1991 Doctor's
Associates Inc"

Subway

Row 1: Explore Space
○ Toy 1: Astronaut
○ Toy 2: Space Station
○ Toy 3: Space Shuttle
○ Toy 4: Lunar Lander
Subway 1994, $4-5 each.
There are variations in paint & decals.
Markings: "Subway ©1994 JGI & DAI Made in China"
Row 2: Hurricanes-4 per set:
○ Toy 1: Amanda
○ Toy 2: Cal
○ Toy 3: Gaston
○ Toy 4: Napper
Subway 1994, $3-5 each.
A TV cartoon series.
Markings: "©1994 JGI & DAI"

Row 3: Inspector Gadget-4 per set:
○ Toy 1: Surprise Squirter
○ Toy 2: Hidden Squirter
○ Toy 3: Stamp Pad-Stamp of Gadget's Face
○ Toy 4: Magnifying Glass
Subway 1994, $3-5 each.
A TV cartoon series.
Markings: "Subway ©1994 JGI & DAI ©1994 DIC Ent LP Made in China"
Row 4: Land of the Lost-4 per set:
〕 Toy 1: Dimetrodon
〕 Toy 2: Triceratops
〕 Toy 3: Stegosaurus
○ Toy 4: Tyrannosaurus Rex
Subway 1993, $2-3 each.
From a TV series, colors may vary.
Markings: "Made in China ACE"

Subway

Row 1: Monkey Trouble-4 per set:
❍ Toy 1: Eva
❍ Toy 2: Eva & Dodger
❍ Toy 3: Dodger
❍ Toy 4: Shorty
Subway 1994, $4-5 each.
A motion picture.
Markings: "©1994 JGI DAI NLP Inc Subway® Made in China"

Row 2: Tall Tale-4 per set & U-3:
❍ Toy 1: Daniel Hackett
❍ Toy 2: John Henry
❍ Toy 3: Pecos Bill
❍ Toy 4: Paul Bunyan
❍ Toy 5: U-3 Paul Bunyan on Babe The Blue Ox
Subway 1995, $4-5 each.
A Disney cartoon motion picture.

Markings: "©Disney Prod for Subway by JGI China"
Row 3: The Santa Clause-4 per set-U-3:
❍ Toy 1: Santa 3-D Puzzle-3 pieces
❍ Toy 2: ELFS Action Figure
❍ Toy 3: Action Snow Globe-twist puzzle
❍ Toy 4: U-3 Comet
❍ Also: Santa Clause Action Figure
Subway 1994, $3-5 each.
A motion picture.
Markings: "Subway ©94 JGI & DAI ©94 Disney"
Row 4: Tom & Jerry-4 per set:
❍ Toy 1: Skateboard Tom
❍ Toy 2: Beach Buggy Jerry
❍ Toy 3: Beach Buggy Tom
❍ Toy 4: Skateboard Jerry
Subway 1994, $3-4 each.
About 2.25" tall.
Markings: "Subway ©1994 TEC Inc ©1994 JGI & DAI"

Taco Bell

Row 1: Congo the Movie Watches-3 per set:
○ Toy 1-3: Congo the Movie Watches
Taco Bell 1995, $5-6 each.
Watches.
Markings: "™ & ©1995 Par Pic Made in China"
Row 2: Mutant Jungle Mix-Ups-6 per set:
○ Toy 1: Red Gorilla & Turquoise Elephant
○ Toy 2: Pink Elephant & Green Rhinoceros
Row 3:
○ Toy 3: Purple Rhinoceros & Turquoise Lion
○ Toy 4: Blue Lion & Violet Wart Hog
Row 4:
○ Toy 5: Orange Wart Hog & Yellow Green
   Crocodile
○ Toy 6: Blue Crocodile & Yellow Gorilla
Taco Bell 1995, $4-5 each.
Two animals per package-two different colors of each animal per set (only six different animals per set-twelve total). Congo the Movie. *Markings:* "Applause PWT"

Subway & Taco Bell & Target Markets

Row 1: Wildlife Rangers-Guard the Animals-
4 per set:
- ○ Toy 1: Stephan, The Snow Leopard
- ○ Toy 2: Herman, The Polar Bear
- ○ Toy 3: Dan, The Lowland Gorilla
- ○ Toy 4: Spot, The Crevy's Zebra

Subway 1993, $3-5 each.
Markings: "Made in China"
Row 2: Busy World of Richard Scarry-2 per set:
- ○ Toy 1: Lowly Worm™
- ○ Toy 2: Heckle Cat™

Taco Bell 1993, $5-8 each.
Finger Puppets-recalled.
Markings: "©1993 Scarry CDM China"
Row 2: Honey, I Blew Up the Kid-1 item:
- ○ Toy 3: Honey, I Blew Up the Kid Disk

Taco Bell 1992, $4-5 each.
A motion picture.
Markings: "©Disney"
Row 2: Rocky & Bullwinkle Stampers-2 per set:
- ○ Toy 4: Bullwinkle-"WOSSAMOTTA U"
- ○ Toy 5: Rocky-"HOKEY SMOKE!"

Taco Bell 1993, $5-7 each.
Stampers.

No Markings
Row 3: Adventure Team Window Walker Figurines-4 per set:
- ○ Toy 1: Bungee Bob
- ○ Toy 2: Freefallin' Freddie
- ○ Toy 3: Rock Climbin' Rochelle
- ○ Toy 4: Tumblin' Tommy

Target Markets 1994, $3-4 each.
Markings: "Patented Made in China"
Row 4: Muppet Twisters-3 per set:
- ○ Toys 1-3: Same muppets, different color blocks

Target Markets 1994, $2-4 each.
Label: "©Henson 1993 Food Avenue® 1993 Target Stores® a Division of the Dayton Hudson Corporation CDM China"
Row 4: Playful Pets-3 per set:
- ○ Toy 4: Martinique the Bichon Puppy
- ○ Toy 5: Fluffy the Kitten
- ○ Toy 6: Max the Dalmatian

Target Markets 1994, $4-5 each.
Snow domes.
Markings: "Food Avenue® 1994 Target Stores® Made in China"

Target Markets & Wal-Mart

Row 1: Targeteers 92-4 per set:
❍ Toy 1: Ashley
❍ Toy 2: Buddy
❍ Toy 3: Danielle
❍ Toy 4: Ramon
Target Markets 1992, $5-6 each.
Legs, heads, and arms move.
Markings: "Copyright ST® (logo)"
Row 2: Targeteers 93-5 per set:
❍ Toy 1: Ashley
❍ Toy 2: Danielle
❍ Toy 3: Mei-Ling
❍ Toy 4: Ramon
❍ Also: Buddy
Target Markets 1993, $4-5 each.
Girls with life-like hair and moving heads, boys with roller blades, moving legs and heads.
Markings: "Made in China"

Row 3: Targeteer's Cars-3 per set:
❍ Toys 1-3: Same car, different colors, Kids not
        included
Target Markets 1992. $4-5 each.
Markings: "ST® (logo) Copyright Reg UK"
Row 3: Targeteer's Skateboard:
❍ Toy 4: Skateboard with Buddy
❍ Also: 3 other Skateboards with Kids
Target Markets 1993, $4-5 each.
No Markings on skateboards
Row 4: Christmas Ornaments-6 per set:
❍ Toy 1: Santa Claus
❍ Toy 2: Mrs Claus
❍ Toy 3: Snowman
❍ Toy 4: Toy Soldier
❍ Toy 5: Elf
❍ Toy 6: Bear
Wal-Mart 1993, $3-5 each.
Printed: "1993 Season's Greetings Shelcore®"

Wal-Mart

Row 1: GI Joe-4 per set:
❍ Toy 1: Awestriker™ & Roadblock™
❍ Toy 2: Persuader™ & Bazooka™
❍ Toy 3: Mobat™ & Grunt™
❍ Toy 4: Warthog™ & Wetsuit™
Wal-Mart 1993, $7-10 each.
About 1.5" tall.
Markings: "©1989 Hasbro Made in China"
Row 2: Lisa Frank-4 per set:
❍ Toy 1: Hollywood Bear™
❍ Toy 2: Markie™
❍ Toy 3: Penguin Surfer™
❍ Toy 4: Sneaker Kitties™
Wal-Mart 1993, $3-4 each.
Also sold retail.
Markings: "©LFI China"
Row 3: Lisa Frank 94-4 per set:
❍ Toy 1: Dolphins
❍ Toy 2: Ballerina Bunny™

❍ Toy 3: Casey™
❍ Toy 4: Panda Painter™
Wal-Mart 1994, $3-4 each.
Also sold retail.
Markings: "©LFI China"
Row 4: Potato Head Kids-4 per set:
❍ Toy 1: Slick
❍ Toy 2: Sabrina
❍ Toy 3: Spike
❍ Toy 4: Tulip
Wal-Mart 1993, $3-5 each.
Also distributed by Avon, Wendy's, and McDonald's.
Markings: "©1986 Hasbro Made in China"
Row 4: Trolls-4 per set:
❍ Toy 5: Troll Necklace
❍ Also: Troll pencil topper, ponytail holder, &
   magnet.
Wal-Mart 1993, $2-3 each.
Trolls also distributed by Hardee's, Long John Silvers, Roy
Rogers, and Sonic.
Markings: "China"

Wal-Mart & Wendy's

Row 1: Shelcore Summer Squirters-6 per set:
- ○ Toy 1: Pelican
- ○ Toy 2: Alligator
- ○ Toy 3: Shark
- ○ Toy 4: Lobster
- ○ Toy 5: Clam
- ○ Toy 6: Frog

Wal-Mart 1994, $2-4 each.
Water Squirters.
Markings: "Summer 1994 ©1994 Shelcore Inc All Rights Reserved Made in China"

Row 2: Alf-6 per set:
- ○ Toy 1: Alf as Robin Hood
- ○ Toy 2: Alf as Little Red Riding Hood
- ○ Toy 3: Alf of Arabia
- ○ Toy 4: Alf as Third Little Pig
- ○ Toy 5: Sir Alf
- ○ Toy 6: Romeo Alf

Wendy's 1990, $3-5 each. A TV series.
Markings: "©1990 Alien Prod Made in China ©1990 Wendy's"

Row 3: Alien Mix-Ups-6 per set:
- ○ Toy 1: Crimson-oid
- ○ Toy 2: Yello-boid
- ○ Toy 3: Spotta-zoid
- ○ Toy 4: Lime-oid
- ○ Toy 5: Blu-zoid
- ○ Toy 6: Purpa-poid

Wendy's 1989, $3-4 each.
Two parts each.
Markings: "©Applause Inc China"

Row 4: All Dogs Go To Heaven-6 per set:
- ○ Toy 1: Carface
- ○ Toy 2: Charlie
- ○ Toy 3: Itchy
- ○ Toy 4: Ann Marie
- ○ Toy 5: Flo
- ○ Toy 6: King Gator

Wendy's 1989, $4-6 each.
A cartoon motion picture.
Markings: "™ ©1989 Goldcrest & Sullivan Bluth Ltd ©1989 Wendy's Int'l Inc China"

Wendy's

Row 1: Arts-5 per set & U-3:
- ○ Toy 1: Hamburger Water Colors
- ○ Toy 2: Red & Purple Frosty Pens
- ○ Toy 3: French Fry Chalk
- ○ Toy 4: Fast Food Crayons
- ○ Toy 5: Hamburger Crayon Puzzle
- ○ Toy 6: U-3 Wendy's Truck

Wendy's 1993, $1 each. #6, $2-5 each.
Markings: "Wendy's ©1993 Wendy's Int'l Inc Made in China"

Row 2: Cybercycles-5 per set:
- ○ Toys 1-5 Cybercycles
- ○ Toy 6: U-3 Cycle

Wendy's 1994, $3-5 each.
Markings: "©1994 Wendy's Int'l China"

Row 3: Definitely Dinosaurs 88-4 per set:

- ○ Toy 1: Apatosaurus
- ○ Toy 2: Anatosaurus
- ○ Toy 3: Triceratops
- ○ Toy 4: Tyrannosaurus Rex

Wendy's 1988, $5-6 each.
About 6" long.
Markings: Definitely Dinosaurs logo

Row 4: Definitely Dinosaurs 89-6 per set:
- ○ Toy 1: Ankylosaurus
- ○ Toy 2: Apatosaurus
- ○ Toy 3: Ceratosaurus
- ○ Toy 4: Parasaurolophus
- ○ Toy 5: Stegosaurus
- ○ Toy 6: Triceratops

Wendy's 1989, $4-6 each.
About 6" long.
Markings: Definitely Dinosaurs logo

Wendy's

Row 1: Dino Games-6 per set:
- Toy 1: Dino Jam Pinball
- Toy 2: Dino Puzzle-3 pieces in case
- Toy 3: Dino Obstacle Course
- Toy 4: Go Fish Dino Cards
- Toy 5: Pterodactyl Egg Catch
- Toy 6: Dino Maze

Wendy's 1992, $3-4 each.
Markings: "Wendy's® Dino Games ©1992 Wendy's Int'l Made in China"

Row 2: Endangered Animal Games-
5 per set & U-3:
- Toy 1: Tiger Pinball
- Toy 2: Sea Turtle Maze
- Toy 3: Eagle Egg Catch Game
- Toy 4: Crazy 8 Animal Cards
- Toy 5: Mini Puzzle
- Toy 6: U-3 Elephant Puzzle-3 pieces

Wendy's 1993, $3-4 each.
The puzzle includes animal-shaped pieces.
Markings: "©1993 Wendy's® China"

Row 3: Food Racers-5 per set:
- Toy 1: Salad Scrambler
- Toy 2: Single Sizzler
- Toy 3: French Fry Rider
- Toy 4: Potato Peeler
- Toy 5: Frosty Flyer
- Toy 6: Kid's Meal

Wendy's 1990, $2-4 each.
Markings: "©1990 Wendy's (logo) ©1990 Determined Prods Made in China"

Wendy's

Row 1: Glass Hangers-9 per set:
- ○ Toy 1: Lion
- ○ Toy 2: Bear
- ○ Toy 3: Gator
- ○ Toy 4: Turtle
- ○ Toy 5: Elephant
- ○ Toy 6: Beaver
- ○ Toy 7: Frog
- ○ Toy 8: Bird
- ○ Toy 9: Pig

Wendy's 1993, $1-2 each.
Also distributed by Sonic.
No Markings

Row 2: Glo Friends-12 per set:
- ○ Toy 1: Bashfulbug
- ○ Toy 2: Bookbug
- ○ Toy 3: Butterfly
- ○ Toy 4: Globug
- ○ Toy 5: Clutterbug
- ○ Toy 6: Cricket

Row 3:
- ○ Toy 7: Doodlebug
- ○ Toy 8: Bopbug
- ○ Toy 9: Grannybug
- ○ Toy 10: Skunkbug
- ○ Toy 11: Snail
- ○ Toy 12: Snugbug

Wendy's 1989, $3-5 each.
Finger puppets.
Markings: "©1986 Playskool Inc Made in China"

Row 4: Glo-Ahead-5 per set & U-3:
- ○ Toy 1: Reusable Stickers
- ○ Toy 2: "Heads will Roll" Pull Back Racer
- ○ Toy 3: Sucker
- ○ Toy 4: Eye Glasses
- ○ Toy 5: Flicker Disks Game
- ○ Toy 6: U-3 Finger Puppet-two sided, boy/girl

Wendy's 1993, $3-5 each.
Glow-in-the-dark.
Markings: "©1993 Wendy's Int'l Inc China"

Wendy's

Row 1: Gobots-5 per set & U-3:
- ◯ Toy 1: Sky Flyer
- ◯ Toy 2: Beamer
- ◯ Toy 3: Pow-Wow
- ◯ Toy 4: Odd Ball
- ◯ Toy 5: U-3 Guide Star
- ◯ Also: Breez-Helicopter

Wendy's 1986, $5-8 each.
Vehicles transform into robots.
Markings: "©Tonka Corp 1985 All Rights Reserved Japan"

Row 2: Good Sports-5 per set & U-3:
- ◯ Toy 1: Pullback Fullback-4 pieces
- ◯ Toy 2: Hockey-4 pieces
- ◯ Toy 3: Golf Game-4 pieces

Row 3:
- ◯ Toy 4: Basketball-6 pieces total
- ◯ Toy 5: Bowling-6 pieces
- ◯ Toy 6: U-3 Baseball

Wendy's 1994, $2-3 each.
Markings: "©1994 Wendy's Int'l Inc China"

Row 4: Goodstuff Gang-6 per set:
- ◯ Toy 1: Wendy
- ◯ Toy 2: Sweet Stuff
- ◯ Toy 3: Lite Stuff
- ◯ Toy 4: Cool Stuff
- ◯ Toy 5: Hot Stuff
- ◯ Toy 6: Overstuff'd

Wendy's 1985, $3-4 each.
Each came in a variety of solid colors.
Markings: "Wendy & The Goodstuff Gang Available exclusively at Wendy's Made in the USA™ & ©HW ©1985 Wendy's Int'l Inc"

Row 4: Happy Moodie
- ◯ Toy 7: Happy Moodie

Wendy's 1984, $6-10
Happy Moodies cast in other colors are rare.
Markings: "©1984 Kent Toys Inc Boyko USA Made in USA"

Wendy's

Row 1: Jetson's Vehicles-6 per set:
- ○ Toy 1: Judy
- ○ Toy 2: Astro
- ○ Toy 3: Jane

Row 2:
- ○ Toy 4: George
- ○ Toy 5: Elroy
- ○ Toy 6: Mr Spacely

Wendy's 1989, $4-5 each.
A TV cartoon series by Hanna-Barbera.
Markings: "©1989 Hanna-Barbera Prod Inc available only at Wendy's® collect all 6 Strottman Int'l Inc Made in China"

Row 3: Jetson's Space Gliders-6 per set:
- ○ Toy 1: George
- ○ Toy 2: Elroy
- ○ Toy 3: Judy

- ○ Toy 4: Astro
- ○ Toy 5: Grunchee
- ○ Toy 6: Fergie

Wendy's 1990, $3-4 each.
A cartoon motion picture.
Markings: "©1990 UCS Jetsons® Property ©H-B Prod Inc Lic by Hamilton Prod Inc Applause™"

Row 4: Mighty Mouse-6 per set:
- ○ Toy 1: Mighty Mouse
- ○ Toy 2: Pearl Pureheart
- ○ Toy 3: The Cow
- ○ Toy 4: Scrappy
- ○ Toy 5: Petey Pate
- ○ Toy 6: Bat Bat

Wendy's 1989, $4-5 each.
On suction cups, Comic book series from the 1940s.
Markings: "™ ©VIACOM Made in China"

Wendy's

Row 1: Potato Head Kids 87-6 per set:
- ○ Toy 1: Rabbit Nubbins
- ○ Toy 2: Blue Mouse
- ○ Toy 3: Big Horn Ram
- ○ Toy 4: Sabrina Witch

Row 2:
- ○ Toy 5: Sir Scallop
- ○ Toy 6: Cavalier

Wendy's 1987, $4-5 each.
Three pieces each, interchangeable. Potato Head Kids were also distributed by Avon, McDonald's, and Wal-Mart.
Markings: "©1987 Hasbro Made in China"

Row 2: Potato Head Kids 88-6 per set:
- ○ Toy 7: Cap'n Kid
- ○ Toy 8: Fireman Sparky
- ○ Toy 8: Fireman Sparky

Row 3:
- ○ Toy 9: Krispy
- ○ Toy 10: Nurse Sophie
- ○ Toy 11: Policeman Duke
- ○ Toy 12: Slugger

Wendy's 1988, $4-5 each.
Three pieces each, interchangeable. Potato Head Kids also distributed by Avon, McDonald's, and Wal-Mart.
Markings: "©1987 Hasbro Made in China"

Row 4: Rocket Writers-5 per set & U-3:
- ○ Toys 1-5 Rocket Writers
- ○ Toy 6: U-3 Explorer 7 Rocket

Wendy's 1992. $2-4 each.
Five novelty writing pens.
Markings: "Wendy's® (logo) ©1992 Wendy's Int'l Inc Made in China"

Wendy's

Row 1: Saurus Sports Balls-4 per set:
- Toy 1: Basketballasaurus
- Toy 2: Baseballasaurus
- Toy 3: Footballasaurus
- Also: Soccerasaurus

Wendy's 1992, $4-5 each.
Markings: "©1986 Talking Tops Made in China"

Row 2: Speed Bumpers-5 per set & U-3:
- Toy 1: BUMP
- Toy 2: FUN
- Toy 3: "CRUSHER"-WOW
- Toy 4: FLY
- Toy 5: "WILD"-WILDTHING
- Toy 6: U-3 "BAG IT!"-BAD

Wendy's 1992, $2-4 each.
Markings: "Wendy's® (logo) ©1992 Wendy's Int'l Inc Made in China"

Row 3: Speed Writers-6 per set:
- Toys 1-6 Speed Writers

Wendy's 1991, $2-4 each.
Novelty pens, over 5" long.
Markings: "Wendy's® (logo) ©1991 Det Prod Made in China"

Row 4: Super Sky Carrier-6 per set:
- Toys 1-3: Super Sky Carrier

Continued in next photo

Wendy's

Row 1: Super Sky Carrier-6 per set-continued from previous photo:

○ Toys 4-6: Super Sky Carrier
Wendy's 1990, $5-6 each.
Each premium can carry a Micro Machines Car (not included), each has peel-off stickers.
Markings: "™ & ©1990 Lewis Galoob Toys Inc Made in China"

Row 2: Techno Tows-4 per set & U-3:
○ Toy 1: Boat Car
○ Toy 2: Shovel Tow
○ Toy 3: 3-Wheeler
○ Toy 4: Tow Truck
○ Toy 5: U-3 Diamond Truck
Wendy's 1995, $2-3 each.
Markings: "©1995 Wendy's Int'l Inc China"

Row 3: Teddy Ruxpin-5 per set:

○ Toy 1: Teddy Ruxpin
○ Toy 2: Wooly What's It
○ Toy 3: Fob
○ Toy 4: Grubby Worm
○ Toy 5: Newton Gimmic-not flocked
Wendy's 1987, $5-7 each.
Flocked.
Markings: "©86 All"

Row 4: Too Cool for School-5 per set & U-3:
○ Toy 1: Hot Numbers Pad
○ Toy 2: Frosty Pencil Sharpener/Eraser
○ Toy 3: Pickle Pen
○ Toy 4: Pencil Pouch with Ruler
○ Toy 5: Hamburger Note Pad
○ Toy 6: U-3 Stencils
Wendy's 1992, $1-2 each.
Markings: "©1992 Wendy's China"

Wendy's

Row 1: Tricky Tints
◯ Toy 1: Tricky Tints Flyer
Wendy's 1992, $5-6 each.
Disk has a 7" diameter. The color changes with sunlight
exposure. Printed: "It Changes Colors"
Row 1: UFO-Unbelievably Fun Objects-
5 per set & U-3:
◯ Toy 1: Satellite Sucker Ball
◯ Toy 2: Squishy Saturn Ball
◯ Toy 3: Glow-in-the-Dark Moon Ball
Row 2:
◯ Toy 4: Comet Ball
◯ Toy 5: Bouncing Planet Ball
◯ Toy 6: U-3 Glow-in-the-Dark Inflatable
      Universe Ball
Wendy's 1992, $4-5 each.
Markings: "©1992 Wendy's China"
Row 3: Wacky Wind-Ups-6 per set:

◯ Toy 1: Christmas Gift Hamburger
◯ Toy 2: Biggie Fries
◯ Toy 3: Miss Baked Potato
◯ Toy 4: Jolly Hamburger
◯ Toy 5: Chocolate Shake
◯ Toy 6: Kid's Meal
Wendy's 1991, $1-3 each.
Wind-Ups.
Markings: "©1991 Wendy's Int'l Inc Made in China"
Row 4: Weird Writers-5 per set & U-3:
◯ Toy 1: Hammer Head
◯ Toy 2: Dizzy
◯ Toy 3: Slimer
◯ Toy 4: Trans-Rex Robot
◯ Toy 5: Surfer
◯ Toy 6: U-3 Boid
Wendy's 1993, $2-3 each.
Markers about 4" tall.
Markings: "©1993 Wendy's Int'l Inc Made in China"

Wendy's

Row 1: Wendy's Toys-2 per set:
- ❍ Toy 1: Football
- ❍ Toy 2: Mini Fun Flyer

Wendy's, $2-3 each.
These items are used as fill-ins between promotions.
Markings: "Wendy's (logo)"

Row 2: Wild Games-5 per set & U-3:
- ❍ Toy 1: Pinball Target
- ❍ Toy 2: Pinball Ski
- ❍ Toy 3: Fries Catch Game
- ❍ Toy 4: Mini Basketball
- ❍ Toy 5: U-3 Soft Ball
- ❍ Also: Fast Food Catch Game

Wendy's 1992, $4-5 each.
Markings: "Wendy's® Wild Games ©1991 Wendy's Int'l Inc Made in China"

Row 3: Write & Sniff-5 per set & U-3:
- ❍ Toy 1: Fireman-Smoke scent
- ❍ Toy 2: Cowboy-Leather scent
- ❍ Toy 3: Beauty Queen-Roses scent
- ❍ Toy 4: Baseball Player-Grass scent
- ❍ Toy 5: Camper-Pine scent
- ❍ Toys 6, 7, & 8: U-3 Stencils

Wendy's 1994, $1-3 each.
Markers with scented ink about 4" tall.
Markings: "©1994 Wendy's Int'l Inc"

Row 4: Yogi Bear & Friends-6 per set:
- ❍ Toy 1: Snagglepuss
- ❍ Toy 2: Cindy
- ❍ Toy 3: Yogi
- ❍ Toy 4: Boo-Boo
- ❍ Toy 5: Ranger Smith
- ❍ Toy 6: Huckleberry Hound

Wendy's 1991, $4-5 each.
Gliders.
Markings: "Available Exclusively at Wendy's ©1990 Hanna-Barbera Prod Inc Lic by Hamilton Projects Inc Mfg by S11 Irvine Ca Made in China"

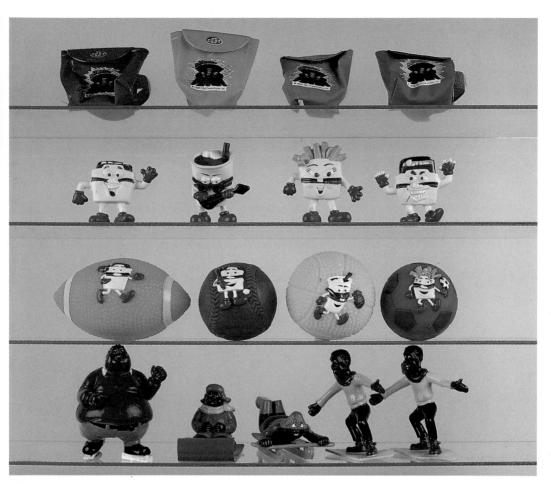

White Castle

Row 1: Captain Planet-4 per set:
❍ Toy 1: Wrist Pack with Decals
❍ Toy 2: Wrist Pack with Magnifier
❍ Toy 3: Wrist Pack with Mirror
❍ Toy 4: Wrist Pack with Compass
White Castle 1995, $1-3 each.
Markings: "©1995 TBS Productions Inc"
Row 2: Castleburger Dudes-4 per set:
❍ Toy 1: Castleburger Dude
❍ Toy 2: Castle Drink Dude
❍ Toy 3: Castle Fry Dudette
❍ Toy 4: Castle Cheeseburger Dude
White Castle 1991, $2-4 each.
Markings: "©1991 White Castle System Inc China"
Row 3: Castleburger Dudes Sports Balls-
4 per set:

❍ Toy 1: Football-Castle Cheeseburger Dude
❍ Toy 2: Baseball-Castleburger Dude
❍ Toy 3: Basketball-Castle Drink Dude
❍ Toy 4: Soccer-Castle Fries Dudette
White Castle 1993, $2-3 each.
Markings: "©1993 White Castle System Inc China"
Row 4: Fat Albert & The Cosby Kids-4 per set:
❍ Toy 1: Fat Albert
❍ Toy 2: Russell
❍ Toy 3: Dumb Donald
❍ Toys 4 & 5: Weird Harold-yellow & white
          sweaters
White Castle 1990, $9-12 each.
A TV cartoon series.
Markings: "©1990 William H Cosby Jr/Filmation Made in
China WHK Enterprises Inc"

White Castle

Row 1: Glow-in-the-Dark Monsters
○ Toy 1: Frankenstein
○ Toy 2: Mummy
○ Toy 3: Wolfman
White Castle 1992, $3-4 each.
About 4" tall.
Markings: "©White Castle 1992 China"
Row 1: Halloween Pez-3 per set:
○ Toy 4: Witch
○ Toy 5: Pumpkin
○ Toy 6: Skull
White Castle 1990, $3-4 each.
About 4" tall.
Markings: "Pez (logo) US Patent 3 942 683 Made in Australia"
Row 1: Nestle Rabbit
○ Toy 7: Nestle Rabbit Straw Slider
○ Also: Spoon, Cup, and Plush
White Castle 1990, $5-12 each.
Markings: "©1990 Nestle® China"

Row 2: Puppy in My Pocket-6 per set:
○ Toys 1-12 Puppy in My Pocket
White Castle 1995, $1-3 each.
Two per package.
Markings: "©MEG 1994"
Row 3: Push N Go Go Go-3 per set:
○ Toy 1: Bulldozer
○ Toy 2: Boat
○ Toy 3: Plane
White Castle 1991, $3-4 each.
Markings: "Tomy® (logo) ©1982 Tomy China"
Row 3: Silly Putty-3 per set:
○ Toys 4-6: No names
White Castle 1994, $1-3 each.
Markings: "Silly Putty® (logo) ©1991 B&S"
Row 4: Stik Mitts-4 per set:
○ Toys 1-4: No names
White Castle 1994, $1-2 each.
Florescent colors.
Printed: "Kid's Castle Meal (logo) White Castle"

White Castle

Row 1: Stunt Grip Geckos-4 per set:
○ Toy 1: Turquoise
○ Toy 2: Purple
○ Also: Mauve & Blue
White Castle 1992, $3-5 each.
Same gecko in four different colors.
Markings: "©1992 White Castle System Inc China"
Row 1: Swat Kats-3 per set:
○ Toy 3: Razor
○ Toy 4: T-Bone
○ Toy 5: Callie
White Castle 1994, $2-3 each.
Two pieces each-launchers behind each Kat, a TV
cartoon series.
Markings: "Swat Kats Radical Squadron™ ©1994 White
Castle System Inc ©Namkung Promotions Inc 1994™ &
©1994 Hanna-Barbera Cartoons Inc"
Row 2: Tootsie Roll Express-4 per set:
○ Toy 1: Engine
○ Toy 2: Gondola

○ Toy 3: Hopper
○ Toy 4: Caboose
White Castle 1992, $5-7 each.
Similar to trains from Dairy Queen and Sonic.
Printed: "White Castle" and "Tootsie Roll Express"
Row 3: Triastic Take-Aparts-4 per set:
○ Toy 1: Mega-saur
○ Toy 2: Spine-asaur
○ Toy 3: Cool-asaur
○ Toy 4: Sora-saur
White Castle 1994, $3-4 each.
Also distributed by Carl's Jr.
Printed: "White Castle®"
Row 4: White Castle Bendy Pens-5 per set:
○ Toy 1: Woozy Wizard
○ Toy 2: Woofles
○ Toy 3: Wobbles
○ Toy 4: Willis
○ Toy 5: Wilfred
White Castle 1993, $4-5 each.
Printed: "White Castle® Castle Meal System Inc ©1992"

White Castle

Row 1: White Castle Food Squirters-3 per set:
- ○ Toy 1: Castle Fry Dudette
- ○ Toy 2: Castleburger Dude
- ○ Toy 3: Castle Drink Dude

White Castle 1994, $4-5 each.
Water squirters.
Markings: "©1994 White Castle System Inc ©Namkung 1994"

Row 2: White Castle Meal Family 89-6 per set:
- ○ Toy 1: Princess Wilhelmina
- ○ Toy 2: Wendell
- ○ Toy 3: Sir Wincelot
- ○ Toy 4: Woozy Wizard
- ○ Toy 5: Woofles
- ○ Toy 6: Willis

White Castle 1989, $5-10 each.
Markings: "©1989 White Castle System Inc Made in China"

Row 3: White Castle Meal Family 92-5 per set:
- ○ Toy 1: Friar Wack
- ○ Toy 2: Wobbles & Woody
- ○ Toy 3: King Woolly & Queen Winnevere
- ○ Toy 4: Wally
- ○ Toy 5: Wilfred

White Castle 1992, $5-10 each.
Markings: "©White Castle System Inc 1992 Made in China"

Row 4: White Castle Meal Family Bubble Makers-4 per set:
- ○ Toy 1: Woozy Wizard
- ○ Toy 2: Princess Wilhelmina
- ○ Toy 3: Wendell
- ○ Also: Sir Wincelot

White Castle 1992, $5-10 each.
Heads unscrew to body bottles & soap bubbles.
Markings: "©White Castle Systems Inc"

Winchell
Simpson Donuts
○ Toy 1: Homer
○ Toy 2: Bart
Winchell's Donut Shops 1993, $7-10 each. Peel-off stickers for messages in English and Spanish, 2 per set.
Markings: "20th Century Fox Made in China Kelston International"

White Castle
Row 1: White Castle Super Balls-4 per set:
○ Toy 1: Castleburger Dude
○ Toy 2: Castle Drink Dude
○ Toy 3: Castle Cheeseburger Dude
○ Toy 4: Castle Fry Dudette
White Castle 1994, $2-3 each.
Super balls with characters in the center. About 1.15" diameter.
Markings: "China"
Printed: "©White Castle 1993"
Row 2: White Castle Water Balls-4 per set:
○ Toy 1: Castle Fry Dudette
○ Toy 2: Castle Cheeseburger Dude

○ Toy 3: Castle Drink Dude
○ Toy 4: Castleburger Dude
White Castle 1993, $2-3 each.
Ball & water inside plastic sphere; Showbiz Pizza also has one with Chuck E Cheese. 1.75" diameter.
Markings: "©1993 White Castle System Inc China"
Row 3: Wind-Up Castleburger Dudes-4 per set:
○ Toy 1: Castle Fry Dudette
○ Toy 2: Castle Cheeseburger Dude
○ Toy 3: Castleburger Dude
○ Toy 4: Castle Drink Dude
White Castle 1992, $2-3 each.
Wind-ups.
Markings: "©1992 White Castle System Inc China"

FOREIGN MARKET
FAST FOOD TOYS

Note: Some of the foreign premiums are identical to the premiums distributed in the US: This section is limited to the premiums that are not identical to the National ones. This section should expand rapidly as more sets are imported and brought back by vacationers. Most of the foreign McDonald's sets are not named. Names were chosen according to their descriptions.

Foreign

Row 1: Aladdin-4 per set:
○ Toy 1: Aladdin & Jasmine-pull back racer
○ Toy 2: Genie in Lamp-twist to raise
○ Toy 3: Sultan Wobble
○ Toy 4: Jafar-arms & attached cloth cape raise
McDonald's Europe 1993, $3-7 each.
Markings: "©Disney China"
Row 2: Aristocats-4 per set:
○ Toy 1: Edgar the Butler on Motorbike
○ Toy 2: Berlioz, Toulouse & Marie in Sidecar-attached to Motorbike
○ Toy 3: O'Malley (short for: Abraham de Lacy Guiseppe Tracy Thomas)
○ Toy 4: Duchess

McDonald's Europe 1994, $3-7 each.
A cartoon motion picture.
Markings: "©Disney China"
Row 3: Astérix™-4 per set:
○ Toy 1: Obelisque
○ Toy 2: Dog
○ Toy 3: Dolphin
○ Toy 4: Astérix™
McDonald's Foreign 1994, $5-10 each. European cartoon character.
Markings: "©1994 GOSCINNY-UDERZO China"
Row 4: Attack Pack-4 per set:
○ Toys 1-4: Attack Pack
McDonald's Canada 1993, $3-4 each.
Markings: "Hot Wheels Mattel (logo)"

Foreign

Row 1: Barbie ?? 4 per set.
- ○ Toy 1: Sea Holiday
- ○ Toy 2: Crystal
- ○ Toy 3: Hollywood Hair
- ○ Toy 4: My First Ballerina

McDonald's Europe 1993, $3-7 each.
Markings: "Made for McDonald's ©1993 Mattel Inc
Made in China"

Row 1: Beauty & The Beast-4 per set:
- ○ Toy 5: Switch Bell
- ○ Also: The Beast, Chip, & Cogsworth

McDonald's Europe 1992, $5-10 each.
Markings: "©1992 McDonald's Corp ©Disney"

Row 2: Dragonettes-4 per set:
- ○ Toys 1-4: Dragonettes

McDonald's Europe 1992, $3-7 each.
Markings: "©McDonald's 1988 China"

Row 3: Euro-Disney-4 per set:
- ○ Toy 1: Chip 'n' Dale in Engine

- ○ Toy 2: Tigger in Tea Cup Ride
- ○ Toy 3: Captain Hook in Ship
- ○ Toy 4: Dalmatian in Fire Engine

McDonald's Europe, $3-7 each.
Markings: "©Disney China"

Row 3: Five Lucky Stars-5 per set:
- ○ Toy 5: Precious
- ○ Also: Bucks, Lucky, Happy, and Richie (all dogs)

McDonald's Orient 1994, $5-7 each.
Markings: "©1994 MCD Corp KY China"

Row 4: Flintstones-4 per set:
- ○ Toy 1: Wilma-Town of Bedrock
- ○ Toy 2: Barney-Bowling-2 pieces
- ○ Toy 3: Fred-Hard Hat Area
- ○ Toy 4: Dino-Bone Diner

Burger King Ltd England 1993, $10-12 each.
Car tops removable.
Markings: "©1993 Hanna-Barbera Prod Inc Burger King
Ltd China"

Foreign

Row 1: Flintstones the Movie-4 per set:
- ○ Toy 1: Wilma & Dino
- ○ Toy 2: Roc Donald's-with 4 sliding wall
     panels with peel-off stickers
- ○ Toy 3: Fred on Brontosaurus
- ○ Toy 4: Bedrock RTD-with peel-off stickers

McDonald's Europe 1994, $3-7 each.
Markings: "The Flintstones™ (logo) ©UCS & Amblin™ H-B
Inc China"
Row 2: Gladiators-6 per set:
- ○ Toys 1-6 Gladiators

Pizza Hut Europe 1992, $10-12 each.

Action figures, like the one shown. Each came with a
combat baton.
No Markings
Row 3: Gliedertiere Floppy Puppet-4 per set:
- ○ Toy 1: Lion
- ○ Toy 2: Elephant
- ○ Toy 3: Dog
- ○ Toy 4: Donkey

McDonald's Europe, $3-7 each.
Push base down to make them "fall apart"
Markings: "CE ©McDonald's Corp Made by Kids
Promotion Grafing"

Foreign

Row 1: Les Animaux de la Jungle-6 per set:
- Toy 1: Ostrich
- Toy 2: Elephant
- Toy 3: Hippo
- Toy 4: Lion
- Toy 5: Giraffe
- Toy 6: Monkey

McDonald's Canada 1992, $3-4 each.
Puzzles, also distributed by Chick-Fil-A.
Markings: "McDonald's"

Row 2: Lion King-4 per set:
- Toy 1: Scar
- Toy 2: Young Nala
- Toy 3: Zazu
- Toy 4: Pumbaa and Timon

McDonald's Europe 1994, $3-7 each.

Wind-Ups. Lion King also distributed by Burger King.
Markings: "©Disney China"

Row 3: Looney Tunes-4 per set:
- Toy 1: Sylvester & Tweety Bird in Airplane
- Toy 2: Bugs Bunny on Scooter
- Toy 3: Daffy Duck in Car
- Toy 4: Wile E Coyote & Road Runner on a Handcart

McDonald's Canada 1989, $3-7 each.
Markings: "Charan Ind ©Warner Brothers Inc 1989 China
©1989 McDonald's China"

Row 3: Los Muppet Bebés en sus Rapimoviles-
4 per set:
- Toy 5: Bebé Rene ("Baby Frog"-Kermit)
- Also: Miss Piggy, Fozzie, and Gonzo

McDonald's Puerto Rico 1992, $5-7 each.
Markings: "MR ©1992 Henson China"

Foreign

Foreign

Row 1: McCharacters-4 per set:
- ○ Toy 1: Grimace
- ○ Also: Ronald, Birdie, and Hamburgular

McDonald's Canada 1985, $7-8 each.
Markings: "McDonald's® ®1985 Made in Canada"

Foreign

Row 1: McAirport-4 per set:
- ○ Toy 1: Ronald's Airplane Service Truck
- ○ Toy 2: Hamburgular's Airplane Service Tractor
- ○ Toy 3: Grimace's Jumbo Jet
- ○ Toy 4: Birdie's Helicopter-2 pieces

McDonald's Europe 1995, $3-7 each.
Markings: "©1995 McDonald's Corp Macau"

Row 2: McBand-4 per set:
- ○ Toy 1: Grimace
- ○ Toy 2: Ronald
- ○ Toy 3: Hamburgular
- ○ Toy 4: Birdie

McDonald's Europe 1993, $3-7 each.
Wind-up for motion.
Markings: "©1993 McDonald's Corp China"

Row 3: McCharacters in Cars, Linkables-4 per set:
- ○ Toy 1: Grimace-2 piece convertible
- ○ Also: Ronald, Birdie, and Hamburgular

McDonald's Europe 1991, $3-7 each.
Markings: "©1991 McDonald's China"

Row 3: McCharacters in Sports Vehicles-4 per set:
- ○ Toy 2: Grimace on Motorized Skateboard
- ○ Toy 3: Birdie on Motorscooter
- ○ Toy 4: Ronald in Racer
- ○ Toy 5: Hamburgular on Jet Ski

McDonald's Europe 1992, $2-5 each.
Markings: "©1992 McDonald's Corp China"

Row 4: McDonald's Akrobat-3 per set:
- ○ Toy 1: Hamburgular
- ○ Toy 2: Birdie
- ○ Toy 3: Ronald

McDonald's Europe, $3-7 each.
Throw them on the wall or window and the sticky feet and hands cling, allowing them to walk down the wall. Similar set distributed by Target Markets- "Adventure Team."
No Markings

Row 4: McDonald's Flyer
- ○ Toy 4: Ronald McDonald's Flyer

McDonald's Canada 1994, $3-5 each.
Markings: "Fabrique au Canada"

Foreign

Row 1: McDonald's Rub & Draw Templates-
2 per set:
○ Toy 1: Ronald
○ Toy 2: Hamburgular
McDonald's Europe 1993, $3-4 each.
Markings: "©1993 McDonald's Corp Simon Marketing Int
Dreieich Made in Italy"
Row 2: McDonald's Summer Fun
○ Toy 1: Bubble Maker Wand
McDonald's Europe 1992, $3-4 each.
Markings: "©1992 McDonald's Corp Simon Marketing Int
Made in Italy"
Row 2: McMeal-1 unit:
○ Toy 2: Tray with Placemat
○ Toy 3: Shake
○ Toy 4: Fries
○ Toy 5: Hamburger

McDonald's Japan, $7-10
Erasers, about 2".
No Markings
Row 3: McMoon Buggies-4 per set:
○ Toy 1: Ronald
○ Toy 2: McRobot
○ Toy 3: Grimace
○ Toy 4: McSpace Shuttle
McDonald's Europe 1995, $3-7 each.
Markings: "©1995 McDonald's Corp China"
Row 4: McRockin' Fast Food-4 per set:
○ Toy 1: Cheeseburger
○ Toy 2: Fries
○ Toy 3: McFish
○ Toy 4: Drink
McDonald's Europe 1991, $3-7 each.
Wind-Ups.
Markings: "©1991 McDonald's Corp Made in China"

Foreign

Row 1: McSpace Rev-Ups-4 per set:
- ○ Toy 1: Birdie
- ○ Toy 2: Ronald's Capsule
- ○ Toy 3: Fry Girl's UFO
- ○ Toy 4: Grimace

McDonald's Europe 1992, $3-7 each.
Markings: "©1992 McDonald's Corp China"

Row 2: McSports
- ○ Toy 1: Ronald on Trampoline
- ○ Toy 2: Birdie Plays Tennis
- ○ Toy 3: Grimace Plays Soccer
- ○ Toy 4: Hamburgular Lifts Weights

McDonald's Europe 1993, $3-7 each.
Turn the rod to make them move, connect together to make them all move together.

Markings: "©1993 McDonald's Corp China"

Row 3: McTown-4 per set:
- ○ Toy 1: Restaurant with Ronald
- ○ Toy 2: Fruit Market with Birdie
- ○ Toy 3: Toy Shop with Grimace
- ○ Toy 4: Fire Station with Fry Guys

McDonald's Europe 1993, $3-5 each.
The detail scenes are peel-off stickers.
Markings: "©1993 McDonald's Corp China"

Row 4: McTransports-4 per set:
- ○ Toy 1: Ronald's Diesel
- ○ Toy 2: Hamburgular's Bus
- ○ Toy 3: Birdie's Hydrofoil
- ○ Toy 4: Grimace's Plane

McDonald's Orient 1993, $3-5 each.
Markings: "©1993 McDonald's Corp"

Foreign

Row 1: McWinter Sports-4 per set:
- ○ Toy 1: Grimace on Snow Tractor
- ○ Toy 2: Ronald on Skis
- ○ Toy 3: Birdie Figure Skating
- ○ Toy 4: Hamburgular in Snow Mobile Pulling Sled

McDonald's Europe 1994, $3-5 each.
Markings: "©1994 McDonald's Corp China"

Row 2: Mr Kiasu-4 per set:
- ○ Toy 1: "Everything also number one!"
- ○ Also: "Everything also I want!," "Everything also want extra!," and "Everything also must grab!"

McDonald's Japan 1993, $3-8 each.
Same character in different poses.
Markings: "©1993 McDonald's Corp China"

Row 2: Olympic McNuggets-? per set:
- ○ Toy 2: Relay Runner

McDonald's Europe 1990, $2-7 each.
Three pieces.
Markings: Arches logo

Row 3: Peanuts-4 per set:
- ○ Toy 1: Snoopy as the Red Baron
- ○ Toy 2: Lucy
- ○ Toy 3: Woodstock
- ○ Toy 4: Charlie Brown

McDonald's Canada 1989, $8-10 each.
Markings: "©1958, 1966 UFS Inc China"

Row 4: Robin Hood Rad Badges-4 per set:
- ○ Toy 1: Sheriff of Nottingham with Robin Hood Wanted Poster
- ○ Toy 2: Maid Marian & Robin Hood
- ○ Toy 3: Little John, Sir Hiss, & Prince John
- ○ Also: One other

Burger King Ltd England 1994, $10-12 each.
A Disney cartoon motion picture.
Markings: "©Disney Made in China"

Foreign
Row 1: Sonic The Hedgehog Sega Zip Strips-
4 per set:
❍ Toy 1: Sonic Canister
❍ Toy 2: Dr Robotnik Gyroscope
❍ Toy 3: Sonic Wheel
❍ Toy 4: Two Tails Flyer
Burger King Ltd Europe 1993, $10-12 each.
Markings: "©Sega Entps Ltd 1991 ©1993 Burger King Ltd
Made in China"
Row 2: Taz Mania Crazies!-4 per set:
❍ Toy 1: Tree Tote Taz Carry Case-3 pieces
❍ Toy 2: Fast Forward Frinzied Taz Pull Back

❍ Toy 3: Tornado Spinner-3 pieces
❍ Toy 4: Wild Wind-Up Wheelie Taz Cycle-
2 pieces
Burger King Ltd England 1993, $10-15each.
Markings: "©1993 Warner Bros Burger King Ltd China"
Row 3: Welcome Year of the Rooster-4 per set:
❍ Toy 1: Wealthy Willy
❍ Toy 2: Healthy Henry
❍ Toy 3: Happy Harry
❍ Toy 4: Lucky Larry
McDonald's Orient 1993, $10-12 each.
Markings: "©1993 McDonald's Corp Made in China"

PLUSH & BIG

Note: Most, but not all, of these plush toys were sold by the restaurants, and not given away with the kid's meals. For convenience of photography, this section also includes the oversized toys. These toys are not in strict alphabetical order. If you collect these plush and big or oversized toys look for them. In general the smaller plush are listed first. Hand puppets are also included here. The name of the set is not necessarily the name of the character - an example of this are the Alf hand puppets, which are listed under the "Many Faces of Alf." Enjoy!

Plush & Big
○ Toy 1: King Burger
Burger King 1970s, $12-20.
Printed fabric, about 13-14" tall.
Printed: "Made in USA"
○ Toy 2: Ronald McDonald
McDonald's 1984, $12-20.
Printed fabric, about 12" tall.
Tag: "Ronald McDonald® ©1984 McDonald's Corp
Group II"

Plush and Big

Plush & Big
Row 1: Aladdin Hidden Treasures
○ Toy 1: Abu
○ Toy 2: Iago
○ Toy 3: Jasmine & Rajah
○ Toy 4: Aladdin & Jasmine
○ Toy 5: Aladdin
Burger King 1994, $1-3 each.
Three pieces each-a box with an inflatable character inside.
Markings: "Disney" and "Burger King Kids Club"

Plush & Big
Row 1: Amazing Wildlife-8 per set:
○ Toy 1: Asiatic Lion
○ Toy 2: Chimpanzee
○ Toy 3: Koala
○ Toy 4: African Elephant
Row 2:
○ Toy 5: Dromedary Camel
○ Toy 6: Galapagos Tortoise
○ Toy 7: Polar Bear
○ Toy 8: Siberian Tiger
McDonald's 1995, $1-3 each.
About 4" tall.
Tag: "National Wildlife Federation® (logo) ©1994

McDonald's Corp"
Row 3: Cinderella-2 per set:
○ Toy 1: Gus
○ Toy 2: Jaques
McDonald's 1987, $7-10 each.
About 3" tall
Row 4: Flintstones-4 per set:
○ Toy 1: Fred & Wilma
○ Toy 2: Barney & Betty
○ Toy 3: Bamm-Bamm & Pebbles
○ Toy 4: Hoppy & Dino
Denny's 1989, $7-10 each.
Two per package, about 3-4" tall.
Tag: "©Hanna-Barbera Productions"

Plush & Big
Row 1: A & W Bear
○ Toy 1: A & W Bear
A & W Drive-ins, $8-12.
About 13" sitting height.
Tag: "Canasia Toys and Gifts Inc Downsview Ontario"
Row 1: After Dark
○ Toy 2: After Dark Flyer
Burger King 1992, $4-5.
Glows-in-the-dark, 9" diameter.
Markings: "Humphery Flyer Made in USA"

Plush and Big

Plush & Big
Row 1: Beauty & The Beast-4
per set:
❍ Toy 1: Beast
❍ Toy 2: Belle
Row 2:
❍ Toy 3: Chip
❍ Toy 4: Cogsworth
Pizza Hut 1992, $5-8 each.
Flexible hand puppets 5-8"
tall.
Markings: "Made in China"

Plush & Big
Row 1: California Raisins III-4
per set:
❍ Toy 1: "Hardee's Soft
Raisin Microphone"
❍ Toy 2: "Hardee's Soft
Raisin Sunglasses"
Row 2:
❍ Toy 3: "Hardee's Soft
Raisin Female Raisin"
❍ Toy 4: "Hardee's Soft
Raisin Conga Dancer"
Hardee's 1989, $5-8 each.
About 6" tall. These are the
third Raisin premiums in the
Kid's Meal.
Tag: "Applause...©1988
CALRAB ...Hardee's"

Plush & Big
Row 1: Alvin & The
Chipmunks-3 per set:
❍ Toy 1: Alvin
❍ Toy 2: Simon
❍ Toy 3: Theodore
Burger King 1987, $7-9
each.
About 10" tall.
Tag: "©1988 Bagdasaria
Productions CBS Toys A
Division of CBS Inc"

Plush & Big
Row 1: Christmas Give-
aways-3 per set:
❍ Toy 1: Chuck E Cheese
Showbiz Pizza 1988, $18-20.
About 12" tall, another
Chuck E is 20" tall.
Tag: "©1988 Showbiz Pizza
Time Inc"
❍ Toy 2: Willis
❍ Also: Woofles and Wilfred
White Castle 1989, $5-7
each.
About 4-5" tall.
Tag: "©1989 White Castle
System Inc"

Plush and Big

Plush & Big
Row 1: Chuck E Cheese
❍ Toy 1: Chuck E Cheese
❍ Toy 2: Jasper
❍ Toy 3: Helen
Showbiz Pizza 1988, $7-8
each.
Tag: "©1988 Showbiz Pizza
Time Inc"
Row 2: Chuck E Cheese
Banks
❍ Toy 1: Chuck E Cheese
❍ Toy 2: Helen
❍ Toy 3: Jasper
Showbiz Pizza 1993, $7-8
each.
PVC banks about 6' tall.
Markings: "©1993 Showbiz
Pizza Time Inc China Dennis
Foland Inc"

Plush & Big
Row 1: Coca-Cola Bear
Hardee's 1993, $10-12
each..
About 8" sitting.
Tag: "Coca-Cola® Brand
Plush Design ©1993 The
Coca-Cola Company"
❍ Toy 2: Dairy Queen Bear
Dairy Queen, $7-8 each.
About 8" tall, has ribbon with
Dairy Queen logos.
Tag: "An Animal Fair Inc®
Product Minneapolis
Minnesota"
Row 2: Crayola Bears-4 per
set:
Burger King 1986, $6-8
each.
About 7" tall.
Tag: "©1986 Graphics
International"

Plush & Big
Row 1: Casper
❍ Toy 1: Casper
❍ Toy 2: Stretch
❍ Toy 3: Fatso
❍ Toy 4: Stinkie
Pizza Hut 1995, $5-6 each.
6-9" tall, glow-in-the-dark
flexible hand puppets. From
the Casper motion picture.
Markings: "Casper ©1995
UCS & Amblin TM Harvey
Made in China"

Plush & Big
Row 1: Eureeka's Castle-3
per set:
❍ Toy 1: Eureeka
❍ Toy 2: Magellan
❍ Toy 3: Batly
Pizza Hut 1990, $5-7 each.
Flexible hand puppets,
about 4-7" tall.
Markings: "Eureeka's
Castle™ ©1990 MTV
Networks Made in China"
Row 2: Furskins-4 per set:
❍ Toy 1: Farrell
❍ Toy 2: Hattie
❍ Toy 3: Dudley
❍ Toy 4: Boone
Wendy's 1986, $6-8 each.
About 6" tall, clothes, hats, &
boots removable.
Tag: "Graphics International
Inc...©1986 Original
Applachian Artwork Inc"

Plush & Big

Row 1: Happy Talk Sprites-4 per set:

◯ Toy 1: Spark

◯ Toy 2: Champ

◯ Toy 3: Twink

◯ Toy 4: Romeo

Taco Bell 1983, $7-8 each.

About 4" sitting, they have a motion squeaker.

Tag: "Made for Taco Bell Graphics International
Inc...©1983 Hallmark Cards Inc Made in China"

Row 2: Hugga Bunch-4 per set:

◯ Toy 1: Gigglet

◯ Toy 2: Fluffer

◯ Toy 3: Hug-A-Bye

◯ Toy 4: Tuggins

Taco Bell 1984, $5-7 each.

About 7" long.

Tag: "Graphics International Inc...©1984 Hallmark Cards
Inc"

Plush & Big

Row 1: Halloween Surprises-4 per set:

❍ Toy 1: Bat in Stump

❍ Toy 2: Ghost in Grocery Bag

❍ Toy 3: Goblin in Kettle

❍ Toy 4: Cat in Pumpkin

Hardee's 1989, $4-6 each.

A plush figure inside a PVC container.

Tag: "Graphics Int's Inc...©1989 Hallmark Cards Inc"

Row 2: Holiday Huggables-4 per set:

❍ Toys 1-3 Holiday Huggables

❍ Also: one other

White Castle 1990, $4-6 each.

About 5" tall.

Toy. "White Castle® ©1990 Graphics International Inc"

Row 3: Little Caesar:

❍ Toy 1: Little Caesar Finger Puppet

Little Caesar's Pizza 1990, $3-5 each.

About 6" tall.

Tag: "©1990 LCE Inc Little Caesars is a Trademark of LCE Inc"

Row 3: Little Mermaid-2 per set:

❍ Toy 1: Flounder

❍ Toy 2: Sebastian

McDonald's 1989, $3-5 each.

3-4" long.

Tag: "©The Walt Disney Company" and the Arches logo

Plush and Big

Plush & Big

Row 1: Land Before Time-6
per set:
❍ Toy 1: Sharptooth
❍ Toy 2: Cara
❍ Toy 3: Duckie
Row 2:
❍ Toy 4: Littlefoot
❍ Toy 5: Spike
❍ Toy 6: Petrie
Pizza Hut 1988, $5-7 each.
Flexible hand puppets, 5-8"
tall.
Markings: "©1988 UCS &
Amblin Made in China"

Plush & Big

Row 1: The Many Faces of
Alf-4 per set:
❍ Toy 1: The Chef
❍ Toy 2: Born to Rock
Musician
Row 2:
❍ Toy 3: Baseball Player
❍ Toy 4: Hawaiian Tourist
Burger King 1988, $8-10
each.
Hand puppets, about 11"
tall.
Tag: "® ©1988 Alien
Productions"

138

Plush & Big
Row 1: Michael Jordan
Fitness Fun-8 per set:
❍ Toy 1: Soccer-inflatable
❍ Toy 2: Baseball
❍ Toy 3: Mini-Football
❍ Toy 4: Mini-Basketball
Row 2:
❍ Toy 5: Disk
❍ Toy 6: Jump Rope
❍ Toy 7: Stopwatch
❍ Toy 8: Waterbottle
McDonald's 1992, $3-5
each.
Markings: "©1991
McDonald's Corp ©Jump
Inc China"

Plush & Big
Row 1: Mickey's Christmas
Carol-5 per set:
❍ Toy 1: Mickey as Bob
Cratchet
❍ Toy 2: Minnie as Mrs
Cratchet
❍ Toy 3: Goofy as Jacob
Marley
Row 2:
❍ Toy 4: Donald as
Scrooge's Nephew Fred
❍ Toy 5: Uncle Scrooge as
Ebeneezer Scrooge
Hardee's 1984, $5-7 each.
About 6" sitting.
Tag: "Mickey's Christmas
Carol...©Walt Disney
Productions"

Plush and Big

Plush & Big

Row 1: Muppet Babies
Christmas Carol-
3 per set:
○ Toy 1: Kermit
○ Toy 2: Miss Piggy
○ Toy 3: Fozzie
McDonald's 1988, $6-7
each.
About 7" sitting, clothes &
hats are removable.
Tag: "©1987 Henson
Associates Inc"
Row 2: Noid:
○ Toy 1: Noid
Domino's Pizza 1994, $6-8
each.
About 10" sitting.
Row 2: Pinocchio Summer
Inflatables-4 per set:
○ Toy 2: Pinochio Beach Ball
(Continued in next photo)

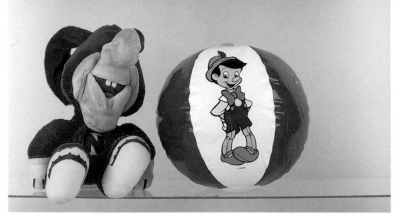

Plush & Big

Row 1: Pinocchio Summer
Inflatables-4 per set:
(continued from previous
photo)
○ Toy 2: Jiminy Cricket Flyer
○ Toy 3: Monstro the Whale
○ Toy 4: Figaro Bobber
Burger King 1992, $2-4
each.
About 7-12", inflatables.
Printed: "©Disney Burger
King Kid's Club (logo)"
Row 2: Pound Puppies 86-4
per set:
○ Toys 1-4: No names
Hardee's 1986 , $3-5 each.
About 7-8" long.
No tags, Pound Puppies logo
on sides.
Row 3: Pur-r-ries & Pound
Puppies 87-5 per set:
○ Toy 1: Kitten
○ Toy 2: Kitten
○ Toy 3: Bulldog
○ Toy 4: Dalmatian
○ Toy 5: Hound Dog
Hardee's 1987, $3-5 each.
About 7-8" long. Others also
sold in stores.
No tags, Pound Puppies logo
on sides

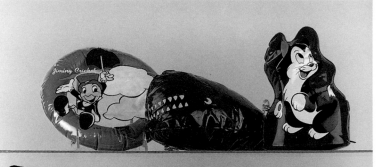

Plush & Big

Row 1: Purr-Tenders-4 per set:
○ Toy 1: Scamp-Purr
○ Toy 2: Hop-Purr
○ Toy 3: Romp-Purr
○ Toy 4: Flop-Purr
Hardee's 1988, $3-5 each.
About 7" tall, these are cats that are pretending to be other animals-see PVCs in Burger King section.
Tag: "Graphics International Inc...©1987 Hallmark Cards"

Row 2: Shirt Tales-5 per set:
○ Toy 1: Rick-"Wild 'n Crazy"
○ Toy 2: Bogey-"Top Banana"
○ Toy 3: Pammy-"Cuddly"
○ Toy 4: Tyg
○ Toy 5: Digger-"Hug Me"
Hardee's 1983, $6-8 each.
About 7: tall, a Hanna-Barbera TV cartoon series.
Tag: "Shirt Tales™"

Plush & Big

Row 1: Mini-Plush Ronald:
○ Toy 1: Ronald
McDonald's 1981, $3-4 each.
Printed: "©1981 McDonald's Corp"
Row 1: Oliver & Company-2 per set:
○ Toy 2: Oliver
○ Toy 3: Dodger
McDonald's 1988, $4-5 each.
About 3-4" tall.
Row 2: Rescuers Down Under-2 per set:
○ Toy 1: Miss Bianca
○ Toy 2: Bernard
McDonald's 1990, $4-5 each.
Flocked, about 3-4" tall.

Row 2: Rudolph
○ Toy 3: Rudolph
McDonald's 1985, $5-7 each.
About 3.5" tall.
Tag: Arches logo & "Coca-Cola (logo)
Row 3: Rodney & Friends-4 per set:
○ Toy 1: Rodney
○ Toy 2: Rhonda
Row 4:
○ Toy 3: Randy
○ Toy 4: Ramona
Burger King 1985, $5-7 each.
About 5" long, Rhonda's red-dotted apron is removable.
Tag: "Graphics International Inc ...©1986 Hallmark Cards Inc"

Plush & Big

Row 1: Shoney Bear-2 per set:
❍ Toy 1: Shoney Bear
❍ Also: Shoney Bear Bank
Shoney's Restaurant 1986, $5-7 each.
Tag: "Shoney Bear"
Row 1: Chuck E Cheese
❍ Toy 2: Chuck E Cheese Drink Container
Showbiz Pizza 1994, $2-3. About 10" tall.
Markings: "©1994 Showbiz Pizza Time Inc Made in Canada"
Row 2: The Simpsons-5 per set:
❍ Toy 1: Homer
❍ Toy 2: Marge
❍ Toy 3: Bart-skateboard tag missing
❍ Toy 4: Lisa
❍ Toy 5: Maggie
Burger King 1990, $4-5 each.
7-12" tall. Krusty the Clown is also available from retail dealers in the same size.
Tag: "Matt Groening The Simpsons™ & ©1990 20th C Fox F C"

Plush & Big

Row 1: Tag Along
❍ Toy 1: Tag Along the Tiger
Sambo's 1978, $40-45 each.
Tag: "Made exclusively for Sambo's© ®Dakin & Co 1978 San Francisco Ca"
Row 1: Walt Disney Classics-5 per set:
❍ Toy 2: Pinocchio
❍ Toy 3: Dumbo
Row 2:
❍ Toy 4: Bambi
❍ Toy 5: Lucky
❍ Toy 6: Lady (& the Tramp)
Hardee's 1985, $6-8 each. About 7" tall.
Tag: "©Walt Disney Productions"

Plush & Big

Row 1: Where in The World is Carmen Sandiego?-5 per set & U-3:

❍ Toy 1: Secret Cup-false bottom
❍ Toy 2: Book/Binoculars
❍ Toy 3: Passport Kit
❍ Toy 4: Ruler/Periscope
❍ Toy 5: Pen/Magnifier
❍ Toy 6: U-3 Attache Case

Wendy's 1994, $1-3 each.
Software program and TV cartoon series.

Markings: "®Broderbund Software Inc Wendy's Int'l Inc China"

Row 2: World Wildlife Fund-4 per set:

❍ Toy 1: Tiger
❍ Toy 2: Panda
❍ Toy 3: Snow Leopard
❍ Toy 4: Koala

Wendy's 1988 $5-8 each.
About 6" tall.

Tag: "World Wildlife Fund ©1988 Determined Productions Inc"

1998 UPDATED

ARBY'S

Row 1: Doodletop Jr
- ○ Toy 1: Blue Huckleberry
- ○ Toy 2: Pink Yogi
- ○ Also: 2 others

Arby's 1996, $1 each. Markers-4 per set. Printed: "CR 1996 Arby's Inc ™ & ©Hanna-Barbera"

Row 2: Junglezoids
- ○ Toy 1: Gorillazoid
- ○ Toy 2: Tigazoid
- ○ Toy 3: Turtazoid
- ○ Toy 4: Rhinozoid

Arby's 1997, $1-2 each-4 per set.
Transformers *Markings:* "©1996 Arby's Inc Made in China"

Row 3: Yogi & Friends Fun Tracer Puzzles
- ○ Toy 1: Ranger Smith-Cindy-Yogi-Boo-Boo
- ○ Toy 2: Huckleberry Hound-Quick Draw McGraw-Baba Loui-Snagglepus

Arby's 1996, $3-4 each-2 per set, 5 pieces each.
Markings: "©1995 Hanna Barbera Productions Inc All Rights Reserved Yogi Bear ™"

Row 4: Yogi & Friends Mix-Match Puzzle
- ○ Toy 1: Top Cat-Breezly-Ricochet Rabbit-Wally Gator
- ○ Toy 2: Yogi-Ranger Smith-Cindy-Snagglepus
- ○ Toy 3: Huckleberry Hound-Hardy Har Har-Lippy the Lion-Quick Draw McGraw

Arby's 1996, $1-2. Twist Puzzles, 3 per set.
Markings: "China" Printed: "©1996 Arby's Inc CR 1996 HBPI All Rights Reserved"

Big Boy
Row 1: Big Boy
○ Big Boy with Hamburger
Big Boy Restaurants 1984,
$5-7
Markings: "© FRI ® RCW
Made in Hong Kong
1984"

Arby's
Row 1: Yogi & Friends Sketch Artists
○ Yogi/Quick Draw McGraw
Also: 2 others
Arby's 1995, $1-2 each. Drawing templates, 3 pieces each, 3 per set.
Markings: "1995 HBPI"
Row 2: Yogi & Friends Snow Domes
○ Toy 1: Snagglepus
○ Toy 2: Cindy
○ Toy 3: Yogi
Arby's 1996, $3-5 each. Snow Domes, 3 per set.
Markings: "©1995 HBPI All Rights Reserved © 1995 Arby's Inc Made in China"
Row 3: Yogi & Friends Spirograms
○ Toy 1: Yogi
○ Toy 2: Boo-Boo
○ Toy 3: Cindy
Arby's 1996, $1-2 each. 2 pieces each in red, yellow, blue and green.
Markings: "Boo-Boo"

Burger King

Row 1: Gargoyles Stone Warriors
❍ Toy 1: Spin-Attack Broadway-3 pieces
❍ Toy 2: Sparkling Spinner Goliath
❍ Toy 3: Spectroscope Brooklyn
❍ Toy 4: Mini-Viewer Lexington
❍ Toy 5: Bronx Launcher-2 pieces
Also: Bucket with Broadway Lid
Burger King 1995, $2-3 each. 6 per set.
Markings: "©BVTV Made in China Burger King Kids Club™ Mfg for Burger King Corp"
Row 2: Glo Force
❍ Toy 1: Boomer-Skier
❍ Toy 2: IQ-Surgeon
❍ Toy 3: Snaps-Camper
❍ Toy 4: Kid Vid-Astronaut
❍ Toy 5: Jaws-Scuba Diver

Burger King 1996, $1-3 each. Glow-in-the-dark Kids with 2 piece costume, 5 per set, 3 pieces each.
Markings: "© 1995 Burger King Corp China"
Row 3: Hunchback of Notre Dame
❍ Toy 1: Frollo
❍ Toy 2: Battle-Action Phoebus
❍ Toy 3: Esmeralda & Djali-2 figurines
❍ Toy 4: Quasimoda
❍ Toy 5: Clopin the Puppeteer-plush
❍ Toy 6: Wacky Hugo
Row 4:
❍ Toy 7: Feather Frenzy Laverne
❍ Toy 8: Winged Victor
Burger King, 1996, $2-4 each. A Disney cartoon motion picture, 8 per set.
Markings: "Manufactured for Burger King Corporation © Disney Made in China"

Burger King
Row 1: m & m Toys
○ Toy 1: Red Inner Tube
○ Toy 2: Orange Dump Truck
○ Toy 3: Yellow Lunch Box
○ Toy 4: Green Car
○ Toy 5: Blue Sax Player
Burger King, 1997, $2-4 each m & m's candy dispensers, 5 per set.
Markings: "Manufactured for Burger King Corporation © Mars Made in China"
Row 2: Oliver & Company 1
○ Toy 1: Sneak-A-Peek Oliver Viewer
○ Toy 2: Dashing Dodger
○ Toy 3: Skateaway Tito
○ Toy 4: Surprise Attack Desoto
Burger King 1996, $1-3 each. A Disney cartoon motion picture, 4 per set.
Markings: "© Disney Manufactured for Burger King Corp Burger King Kid's Club (logo) Made in China"
Row 3: Oliver & Company 2

○ Toy 1: Pop-Up Roscoe and Desoto
○ Toy 2: Scampering Tito
○ Toy 3: Floating Jenny and Oliver-2 pieces
○ Toy 4: Speeding Scooter
○ Toy 5: Chomping Dodger
Burger King 1996, $1-3 each. A Disney cartoon motion picture, 5 per set.
Markings: "© Disney Mfg for Burger King Corp Inc China"
Row 4: Pocahontas
○ Toy 1: Chief Powhatan
○ Toy 2: Pocahontas
○ Toy 3: Captain John
○ Toy 4: Governor Ratcliffe
○ Toy 5: Percy
○ Toy 6: Meeko
○ Toy 7: Grandmother Willow
○ Toy 8: Flit
Burger King 1995, $3-4 each. A Disney cartoon motion picture, 8 per set.
Markings: "© Disney Mfg for Burger King Corp China"

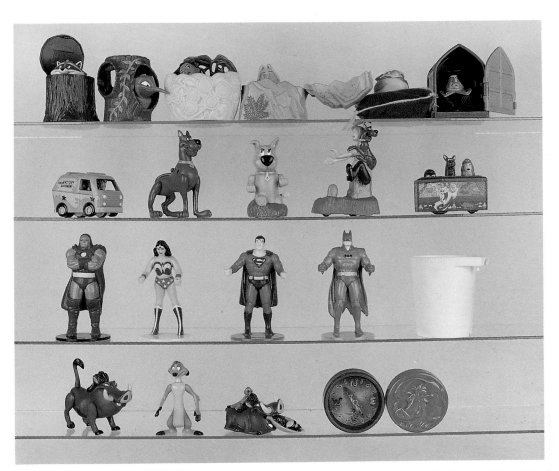

Burger King

Row 1: Pocahontas Hide 'n' Seek Finger Puppets
○ Toy 1: Meeko's Hideout
○ Toy 2: Busy Body Flint
○ Toy 3: Peek-A-Boo Pocahontas
○ Toy 4: John Smith's Lookout
○ Toy 5: Pampered Percy-plush
○ Toy 6: Ruthless Ratcliffe
Burger King 1996, $1-2 each-6 per set.
Markings: "Burger King Kid's Club (logo) Manufactured for Burger King Corporation © Disney"
Row 2: Scooby-Doo
○ Toy 1: The Mystery Machine Bus
○ Toy 2: Scooby Doo
○ Toy 3: Scrappy Doo
○ Toy 4: Shaggy & Scooby Doo
○ Toy 5: Velma, Scooby, and Daphne
Burger King 1996, $4-8 each. Hanna-Barbera TV cartoons, 5 per set.

Markings: "™ & © Hanna-Barbera Mfg for Burger King Corp"
Row 3: Super Powers Cup Holder Collection
○ Toy 1: Darkseid
○ Toy 2: Wonder Woman
○ Toy 3: Superman
○ Toy 4: Batman
○ Toy 5: Cup
Burger King 1988, $6-10 each. Each hero holds a drinking cup like the cup shown, 4 per set, 2 pieces each.
Markings: "Darkseid is a Trademark of DC Comics Inc ©1988 Figurine Cupholder Created by Robert Demars Pat Pend"
Row 4: Timon & Pumbaa
○ Toy 1: Pumbaa
○ Toy 2: Timon
○ Toy 3: Bug Munchin' Pumbaa
○ Toy 4: Super Secret Compass
Burger King 1996, $1-3 each. Disney TV cartoons, 4 per set.
Markings: "© Disney Mfg for Burger King Corp"

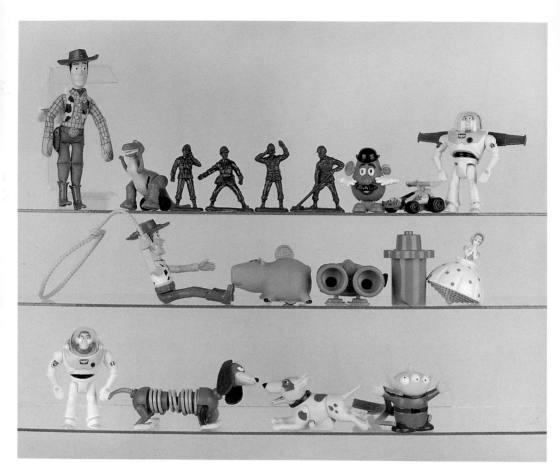

Burger King
Row 1: Toy Story 95
❍ Toy 1: Woody-plush
❍ Toy 2: Rex
❍ Toy 3: Army Recon Squad-4
❍ Toy 4: Mr Potato Head-wind-up
❍ Toy 5: RC Racing Car
❍ Toy 6: Buzz Lightyear
Burger King 1995, $3-5 each. A Disney motion picture, 6 per set.
Markings: "© Disney Made in China ©Pixar Mfg for Burger King Corp"
Row 2: Toy Story 96

❍ Toy 1: Woody
❍ Toy 2: Hamm
❍ Toy 3: Lenny
❍ Toy 4: Bo Peep-2 pieces
Row 3:
❍ Toy 5: Buzz Lightyear
❍ Toy 6: Slinky
❍ Toy 7: Scud
❍ Toy 8: Alien & The Claw-2 pieces
Burger King 1996, $3-6 each. A Disney motion picture, 8 per set.
Markings: "© Disney Mfg for Burger King Corp Burger King Kid's Club (logo)"

Carl's Jr.

Row 1: Bobby's World
○ Toy 1: Bobby's Silly Scrambler-twist puzzle
○ Toy 2: Wacky Webby-suction
Also: Rollin' Roger in Wagon & Bobby's Double-Duty Dozer
Carl's Jr 1996, $2-5 each-4 per set. Printed: "(star) Carl's Jr (logo) ©1996 Carl Karcher Enterprises Inc"
Row 2: Eek! The Cat
○ Toy 1: Eek! The Cat
Also: Annabelle & Sharky
Carl's Jr 1995, $2-5 each. A TV cartoon series
Markings: "Edkstravaganza ™ ©1995 FCN © Carl Karcher Ent Inc 1995 ©Namkung 1995 China Carl's Jr ® (logo)"
Row 2: Key Racers
○ Toy 2: Blue
Also 3 others
Carl's Jr 1994 $1-3 each
Markings: "Carl's Jr ® (logo) Key Racers ™ © Carl Karcher Ent Inc 1994 CR Namkung 1994 China"
Row 2: Monsters
○ Toy 3: Monster

Also 3 others
Carl's Jr 1988 $3-5 each
Markings: "Dist by Carl Karcher Ent Inc 1988"
Row 2: Pencil Toppers
○ Toy 4: Skeleton Boy
Also 3 others
Carl's Jr 1995 $1-3 each
Markings: "Carl's Jr ®©Carl Karcher Ent Inc 1995 © NPI 1995 China"
Row 3: The Chipmunks Snow Domes
○ Toy 1: Alvin
○ Toy 2: Theodore
○ Toy 3: Simon
Carl's Jr 1994, $3-5 each. Snow domes, 3 per set.
Markings: "(star) Carl's Jr © (logo) Carl Karcher Ent Inc 94 ™ & © 1994 Bagdasarian Prod"

Checkers
Row 4: Creatures
Checkers 1995, $2-3 each
Markings: "© 1995 Checkers Drive In Restaurants Inc"

Chick-Fil-A

Row 1: Colors of the World
○ Toy 1: Camel
○ Toy 4: Giant Anteater
○ Toy 2: Musk Ox
○ Toy 5: Cottontail
○ Toy 3: Wart Hog
○ Toy 6: Polar Bear
Chick-Fil-A 1997, $1-3 each. Water color paint sets, 6 per set.
Markings: "Chick-Fil-A ® (logo) © Chick-Fil-A ® Inc August 1996 ©Namkung Promotions Inc 1996 China"
Row 2: Global Gushers
○ Toy 1: Camel
○ Toy 3: Snake
○ Toy 2: Ape
○ Toy 4: Koala
Chick-Fil-A 1995, $2-4 each. Plunger squirters, 4 per set.
Markings: "Chick-Fil-A ® (logo) Chick-Fil-A Inc ®1995 ©NPI 1995"
Row 3: Global Mobiles
○ Toy 1: Steam Locomotive
○ Toy 4: Gondola
○ Toy 2: Airplane
○ Toy 5: Elephant
○ Toy 3: Off-Road Vehicle

Chick-Fil-A 1995, $2-4 each. Details are peel-off stickers, 5 per set
Markings: "Chick-Fil-A ® (logo) Chick-Fil-A Inc 1995"
Row 4: Houses Around the World
○ Toy 1: Ice Station-Antarctica
○ Toy 2: Steppe House-Asia
○ Toy 3: Adobe Hut-South America
○ Toy 4: Sheep Station-Australia
○ Toy 5: Log Cabin-North America
○ Toy 6: Grass Hut-Africa
○ Toy 7: Castle-Europe
Chick-Fil-A 1995, $2-4 each. Houses are viewers, each sits on it's continent, 7 per set, 2 pieces each.
Markings: "Chick-Fil-A ® (logo) Chick-Fil-A Inc ® 1995 ©CDM Made in China"

Chick-Fil-A

Row 1: International Kids
○ Toy 1: Pilar
○ Toy 3: Idris
○ Toy 2: Heidi
○ Toy 4: Tigluk
Also: 3 others
Chick-Fil-A 1995, $2-4 each-7 per set.
Markings: "Chick-Fil-A ® (logo) Chick-Fil-A Inc ® 1995 Namkung Inc 1995 China"
Row 2: Wonderful World of Landmark Planters
○ Toy 1: The Castillo
○ Toy 2: The Guggenheim Museum
Also: The Emperor's Palace, The Great Spinx, The Colosseum, and The Mexican Pyramid
Chick-Fil-A 1996, $2-4 each. Little planting pots, 6 per set.
Markings: "Chick-Fil-A ® (logo) Chick-Fil-A Inc 1995 Namkung 1995"

Dairy Queen

Row 1: Beethoven
○ Toy 1: Beethoven
○ Toy 2: Caesar
○ Toy 3: Sparkey
○ Toy 4: Spot
○ Toy 5: Beethoven Squirter
Dairy Queen 1996, $2-4 each. A TV cartoon series, 5 per set.
Markings: "™ & © 1995 UCS Made in China"
Row 2: Bendy Dinosaurs
○ Toy 1: Brachiosaurus
○ Toy 2: Triceratops
○ Toy 3: Velocirapics
Dairy Queen 1995, $1-3 each-5 per set.
Marking: "Made in China © 1993 CE (logo) "
Row 3: Bio-Karts

○ Toy 1: Dennis in Soapbox Kart
○ Toy 2: Joey in Fire Truck
Also: Margaret with Baby Buggy & Ruff in Red Wagon
Dairy Queen 1997, $2-3 each-4 per set.
Markings: "Dennis The Menace Bio-Karts Dairy Queen (logo)
© Katchem ® ™ of Am DQ Corp © 1996 Am DQ Corp Mpls
MN"
Row 4: Bobby's World
○ Twist Puzzle
Also: others
Dairy Queen 1995, $1-2 each. Printed: "All Rights Reserved ®
™ Am DQ Corp © 1995 Am DQ Corp Mpls Mn © 1995 CDM"
Row 5: Circus Stackers
○ 5 Stacking Animals
Dairy Queen 1996, $1-2 each.
No markings.

153

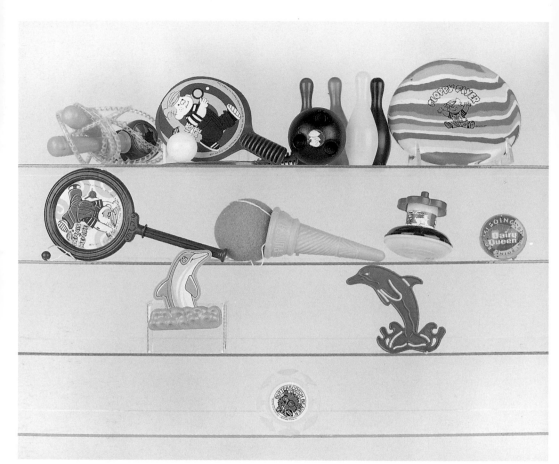

Dairy Queen

Row 1: Dennis Sports Equipment
◯ Toy 1: Jumprope
◯ Toy 2: Ping Pong
◯ Toy 3: Bowling Game
◯ Toy 4: Floppy Flyer
Row 2:
◯ Toy 5: Drum Ball Game
◯ Toy 6: Ice Cream Cone Punch-recalled
◯ Toy 7: Top
◯ Toy 8: Superball
Dairy Queen 1996, $1-4

Markings: "Dairy Queen"
Row 3: Dolphin Fun
◯ Toy 1: Dolphin Clip
◯ Toy 2: Dolphin Rub-On Stencil & Bookmark
Also: Dolphin Press (stamper) & Dolphin Sticker Dispenser
Dairy Queen 1996, $1-3 each-4 per set.
Markings: "Dairy Queen (logo) ® ™ Am DQ Corp ©1996 Am DQ Corp Mpls Mn"
Row 4: DQ Spinner
◯ Butterscotch Spinner
See page 34 for the set information

154

Dairy Queen

Row 1: Freaky Friends
○ Toy 1: Light Blob
○ Toy 2: Spinning Bat
○ Toy 3: Tumble Spider
Also: Inflate-An-Alien
Dairy Queen 1996, $1-2 each-4 per set.
Markings: "Dairy Queen ® (logo) ® ™ Am DQ Corp © 1996 Am DQ Corp Mpls MN Made in China"
Row 2: Fun Pals
○ Toy 1: Bearly Bob Pencil Holder
○ Toy 2: Waddles-Penguin
○ Toy 3: Smilosaurus-3 pieces
○ Toy 4: Waddles-Beaver
○ Toy 5: Pencil Holder
Also: Popalong-2 pieces
Dairy Queen 1996, $1-3 each-4 per set.
Markings: "® ™ Am DQ Corp © 1995 Am DQ Corp Mpls MN"
Row 3: Kidsville Kids

○ Toy 1: Ricky
○ Toy 2: Julie
○ Toy 3: Angela
○ Toy 4: Brian
Dairy Queen 1997, $2-4 each. Similar to Targeteers, however they are holding Coke Cups while the Kidsville Kids have DQ drinks, 4 per set, also 2 cardboard buildings in the offering.
Markings: "Made in China"
Row 4: Magic School Bus
○ Toy 1: Bus Puzzle
○ Toy 2: Bus Blaster
○ Toy 3: Music Maker
○ Toy 4: Pencil Pouch
Dairy Queen 1996, $2-3 each-4 per set.
Markings: "The Magic School Bus (logo) Dairy Queen (logo)"
Row 5: Moon Ball
○ Squish Ball
Dairy Queen 1995, $2-4 each
No markings

Dairy Queen

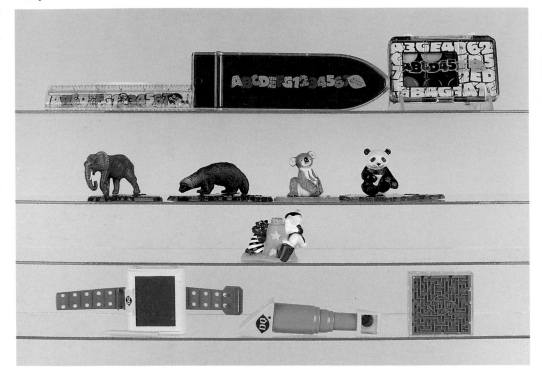

Dairy Queen
Row 1: School Supplies
❍ Toy 1: Ruler/Glitter Wand
❍ Toy 2: Pencil Box
❍ Toy 3: Water Colors
Dairy Queen 1995, $2-4 each-3 per set.
Markings: "© & ™ Am DQ Corp Dairy Queen (logo)"
Row 2: National Wildlife
❍ Toy 1: Elephant-Africa
❍ Toy 2: Wolverine-Europe
❍ Toy 3: Koala-Australia
❍ Toy 4: Panda-Asia
Also: Grisley-NA, Panther-SA, Penguin-Antartica

Dairy Queen 1997, $2-3 each-7 per set, 2 pieces each-animal and continent.
Markings: "©1996 NWF ©1996 CDM 96220 China"
Markings on Continents: "Dairy Queen ® (logo) National Wildlife Federation ® (logo) CR 1996 National Wildlife Federation"
Row 3: Squirters
❍ Cat & Dog on Sand Castle

Also: Tropical Fish
Dairy Queen 1996, $1-3 each.
Markings: "© PPG 1996 China"
Row 4: Treatmeal
❍ Toy 1: Wrist Magic Slate
❍ Toy 2: Periscope
❍ Toy 3: 3-D Maze Puzzle
Dairy Queen 1996, $1-3 each
No markings

Dennys
Row 1: Jetson Planet Balls
❍ Toy 1: Mars
❍ Toy 2: Moon
See page 39 for the set information
Discovery Zone
Row 2: Discovery Zone
❍ Slide Puzzle
Discovery Zone 1995, $1-2
Markings: "Made in China"
Domino's PizzA
Row 3: Cool Dude Domino
❍ Toy 1: Cool Dude

Domino's Pizza 1994, $3-4
Markings: "©1993 Domino's Pizza Inc Safety Tested for Children 3 and Older Made in China"
Domino's Pizza
Row 3: Playing Cards
❍ Toy 2: Domino's Playing Cards
Domino's Pizza 1995, $3-5.
Printed: "Domino's Pizza (logo) Domino's Pizza Delivers ™ Free"

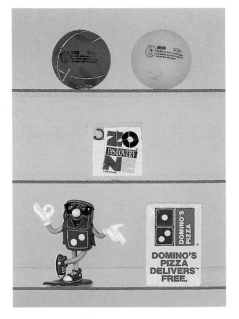

Hardee's

Row 1: Balto
○ Toy 1: Rosie
○ Toy 2: Boris & Balto
○ Toy 3: Muk-finger puppet
○ Toy 4: Luk-finger puppet
○ Toy 5: Jenna & Rosie
○ Toy 6: Balto
Hardee's 1996, $2-4 each. A cartoon motion picture, 6 per set.
Markings: "©1995 USC & Amblin 1995"
Row 2: Bobby's World
○ Toy 1: Bobby
○ Toy 2: Webby
○ Toy 3: Roger
○ Toy 4: Uncle Ted
○ Toy 5: Captain Squash
Hardee's 1996, $2-4 each. ATV cartoon series, 6 per set.
Markings: "™ & © 1996 FCN 1996 Hardee's Dakin/China"
Row 3: Doodletop Jr
○ Doodletop Jr
Hardee's 1996, $1 each-4 per set. Printed: "Hardee's © 1995 Hardee's Food System Inc"
Row 4: Homeward Bound II
○ Toy 1: Riley
○ Toy 2: Chance
○ Toy 3: Sassy
○ Toy 4: Shadow
○ Toy 5: Delilah
Hardee's 1996, $2-4 each. A motion picture, 5 per set, 2 pieces each.
Markings: "© Disney 1996 Hardee's Dakin/China"

Hardee's

Row 1: Humming Birds
○ Toy 1: Toot-Can
○ Toy 2: Humm-Dinger
○ Toy 3: Para-Tweet
○ Toy 4: Horn-Bill
Hardee's 1995, $2-4 each. "Kooky,
Koo-Koo Kazoos!" 4 per set.
Markings: "©1995 Chuck Kennedy
1995 Hardee's Dakin/China"
Row 2: Micro Super Soaker
○ Toy 1: Water Blaster
○ Toy 2: Micro XP
○ Toy 3: Power Pump
○ Toy 4: Super Saturator
Also: Power Soaker & Soak 'n' Fly
Hardee's 1995, $1-2 each. Squirters, 6
per set.
Markings: "© 1995 Larami Corp Lic by
LCI Inc © 1995 Hardee's Food Systems
Inc Made in China"
Row 3: Nickelodeon School Tools
○ Toy 1: Spunky ™ Container
○ Toy 2: Krumm ™ Paper Clip
○ Toy 3: Rocko ™ Ruler
○ Toy 4: Ickis ™
○ Toy 5: Oblina ™ Pencil Topper

○ Toy 6: The Gromble ™ Container
Hardee's 1995, $2-4 each. Each
came with a Pog, 6 per set.
Markings: "© 1995 Nickelodeon
Hardee's/Dakin China"
Row 4: Wild Wonders
○ Toy 1: Elephant Squirter
○ Toy 2: Flow-Spot Leopard
○ Toy 3: Tiger Stamper-"a paw print"
○ Toy 4: Stick-On Gorilla
Hardee's 1996, $2-3 each-4 per set.
No markings

Right: Hardee's
Row 1: Dinos
○ Rex
See page 43 for the set information
Row 2: Food Squirter
○ Hot Dog
See page 44 for set information
Row 3: X-Men
○ U-3 Wolverine
See pages 49 and 88 for set
information

International House of Pancakes

Row 1: Pancakes Kids on Skateboards

❍ Chocolate Chip Charlie

Also: others

International House of Pancakes 1996, $4-5 each

Markings: "©1996 Int'l House of Pancakes Inc Made in China"

Jack-in-The-Box

Row 2: Jack's Pack Bendables

❍ Toy 1: Jack with Briefcase

❍ Toy 2: Jack with Remote Control

❍ Toy 3: Jack with Hamburger

Jack-in-The-Box 1996, $3-5 each-3 per set.

Markings: "Jack-in-The-Box ® (logo) Made in China"

K-Mart

Row 3: Rainbow Coil

❍ Coil

K-Mart 1996, $2-4 each, single offering.

No markings

Row 4: Toy Story Slide Puzzle

❍ Toy 1: Hamm

❍ Toy 2: Rex

❍ Toy 3: Woody

❍ Toy 4: Buzz

❍ Toy 5: Bo Peep

❍ Toy 6: Alien

K-Mart 1996, $3-5 each-6 per set.

Markings: "©Disney"

Kentucky Fried Chicken

Row 1: Casper

○ Toy 1: Poil
○ Toy 2: Casper
○ Toy 3: Spooky
○ Toy 4: Stretch
○ Toy 5: Fatso
○ Toy 6: Stinkie

Kentucky Fried Chicken 1996, $3-4 each. Glow-in-the-Dark squirters, 6 per set.

Markings: "©1996 Universal/Harvey ™ Made in China"

Row 2: Eek! The Cat

○ Toy 1: Ka-Boooom! Annabelle-2 pieces
○ Toy 2: Eek Balancing Act
○ Toy 3: Sharky's Dog House Launcher-2 pieces
○ Toy 4: Kutter Copter-2 pieces
○ Toy 5: Cool Doc Moves

Kentucky Fried Chicken 1996, $2-4 each. A TV cartoon series. 5 per set.

Markings: "Eek! ™ Strava Ganza ™ & © 1996 Fox Childrens Network Inc Made in China Equity Promotions"

Row 3: Garfield 500

○ Toy 1: Off Road Odie
○ Toy 2: Cruisin' Jon
○ Toy 3: Warp Speed Pooky
○ Toy 4: Chug-a-Long Nermal
○ Toy 5: Airborn Arlene

Also: Grand Prix Garfield

Kentucky Fried Chicken 1996, $3-5 each. A TV cartoon series, 6 per set.

Markings: "©1996 PAWS Made in China"

Row 4: Linkbots

○ Toy 1: Quad
○ Toy 2: Ros
○ Toy 3: Keed
○ Toy 4: R-M
○ Toy 5: Orj
○ Toy 6: Awz

Kentucky Fried Chicken 1995, $3-5 each. Can link together, 6 per set.

No markings

Row 5: Masked Rider

○ Toy 1: Masked Rider Super Gold-2 pieces
○ Toy 2: Bump & Go Ferbus
○ Toy 3: Press & Go Super Chopper
○ Toy 4: Magno The Super Car
○ Toy 5: Glow-in-the-Dark X-Ray Cyclopter
○ Toy 6: Ecto Viewer Wrist Band-2 pieces

Kentucky Fried Chicken 1997, $2-4 each. TV series, 6 per set.

Markings: "TM & CR 1997 Saban Made in China Discovery Concepts"

Kentucky Fried Chicken
Timon & Pumbaa
○ Toy 1: Snail Snackin' Timon
○ Toy 2: Bug Muchin' Pumbaa
○ Toy 3: Out-to-Lunch Timon
○ Toy 4: Hawaiian Luau Pumbaa
○ Toy 5: Jungle River-Riding Timon
○ Toy 6: Bug Bath Pumbaa
Kentucky Fried Chicken 1996, $2-4 each. A TV cartoon series,
6 per set.
Markings: "© Disney Made in China Equity Promotions Los
Angeles Ca"

Krystal
Row 1: Krystal Country
○ Toy 1: Hot Dog Drummer
○ Toy 2: Krystal on Guitar
○ Toy 3: Corn Pup on Keyboard
○ Toy 4: Kool Drink on Sax
○ Toy 5: Singing Fries

Krystal 1996, $3-5 each-6 per set.
Markings: "©1995 Krystal (logo) China"
Row 2: Sportsballs
○ Toy 1: Basketball
○ Toy 2: Football
○ Toy 3: Soccerball
Krystal, $1-2 each-3 per set. Printed: "Krystal ® (logo)"

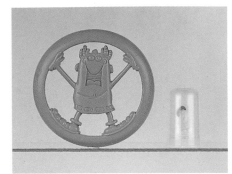

Little Caesar's Pizza
Row 1: Little Caesar
○ Toy 1: Flyer
○ Toy 2: Water Ring Catch
Little Caesar's Pizza 1994, $2-4 each
Markings: "©1994 LCE Inc China"

Long John Silvers
Row 1: Free Willy 2
○ Toy 1: Jesse
○ Toy 2: Little Spot
○ Toy 3: Luna
○ Toy 4: Willy
Long John Silvers 1995, $3-5 each. A
motion picture, 4 per set.
Markings: "Free Willy ™ Warner Bros China"
and whales name on belly
Row 2: Peanuts Christmas Boxes
○ Toy 1: Snoopy
○ Toy 2: Charlie Brown
○ Toy 3: Sally
○ Toy 4: Lucy

Long John Silvers 1996, $2-5 each-4 per set.
Markings: "Peanuts © UFS Inc Made in China
by Equity Promotions ™"
Row 3: The Disney Channel
○ Toy 1: Goofy
○ Toy 2: Baloo
○ Toy 3: Dale
Also: Uncle Scrooge
Long John Silvers 1997, $2-4 each. Straw
sliders, 4 per set.
Markings: "CR Disney China"
Row 4: Water Blasters
○ Ophelia Octopus
See page 53 for the set information

McDonald's

Row 1: 101 Dalmatians
❍ Toy 1: Dalmatian Puppy
McDonald's 1996, $2-3 each. A Disney cartoon motion picture, 101 different puppies per set.
Markings: "© Disney China"
Row 1: 101 Dalmatians Snow Domes
❍ Toy 2: Movie Title
❍ Toy 3: Dome
❍ Toy 4: Snowman
❍ Toy 5: Sled
McDonald's 1996, $3-5 each. A Disney cartoon motion picture, 4 per set.
Markings: "© Disney Made for McDonald's ® China"
Row 2: Aladdin & The Forty Thieves

❍ Toy 1: Cassim/Falcon
❍ Toy 2: Abu & Carpet/Castle
❍ Toy 3: Jasmine/Balcony
❍ Toy 4: Iago/Treasure Chest
Row 3:
❍ Toy 5: Genie/Market
❍ Toy 6: Saluk/Cave
❍ Toy 7: Aladdin/Palace Interior
❍ Toy 8: Matre D' Genie/Restaurant
Row 4:
❍ Toy 9: U-3 Abu
McDonald's 1996, $1-2 each. A Disney cartoon motion picture, 8 per set & U-3.
Markings: "© Disney China/Chine"

McDonald's

Row 1: Animaniacs
- ○ Toy 1: Pinky & The Brain
- ○ Toy 2: Goodfeathers
- ○ Toy 3: Dot & Ralph
- ○ Toy 4: Wakko & Yakko
- ○ Toy 5: Slappy & Skippy

Row 2:
- ○ Toy 6: Mindy & Buttons
- ○ Toy 7: Wakko, Yakko, & Dot
- ○ Toy 8: Hip Hippos
- ○ Toy 9: U-3 Trio

McDonald's 1995, $1-2 each. A TV cartoon series, 8 per set & U-3.

Markings: "™ & © 1994 Warner Bros China Chine"

Row 3: Barbie 95
- ○ Toy 1: Hot Skatin' Barbie-Barbie Roulettes Magiques-Barbie Patines Magicas
- ○ Toy 2: Dance Moves Barbie-Barbie Je Danse-Barbie Baila Y Gira-2 pieces
- ○ Toy 3: Butterfly Princess Teresa-Teresa Princess Papillon-Teresa Princesa de Mariposa
- ○ Toy 4: Cool Country Barbie-Barbie Equestre-Barbie Estilo Country
- ○ Toy 5: Lifeguard Ken-Ken Super Sauvetage-Ken Salve-Vidas-2 pieces
- ○ Toy 6: Lifeguard Barbie-Barbie Super Sauvetage-Barbie Salve-Vidas-2 pieces
- ○ Toy 7: Bubble Angel-Bulles Enchatees-Burbujas Magicas
- ○ Toy 8: Ice Skatin'-Patins a Glace-Patinado
- ○ Toy 9: U-3 Jouet Pour Moins de 3 Ans-Menores de 3 An*os Premio

McDonald's 1996, $2-5 each. The multiple language packaging was started with this set, 8 per set & U-3.

Markings: "© 1994 Mattel Inc China"

McDonald's

Row 1: Barbie 96

○ Toy 1: Dutch Barbie-Hollandaise-Holandesa
○ Toy 2: Kenyan Barbie-Kenyenne-Keniana-2 pieces
○ Toy 3: Japanese Barbie-Japonaise-Japonesa-2 pieces
○ Toy 4: Mexican Barbie-Mexicaine-Mexicana
○ Toy 5: USA Olympic Barbi-Americaine-Americana-2 pieces
○ Ioy 6: U-3 Puzzle Slide Barbie

McDonald's 1996, $2-3 each. "Hair" and cloth clothes, 5 per set & U-3.

Markings: "© 1995 Mattel Inc China"

Row 2: Eric Carle

○ Toy 1: The Very Quiet Cricket- Le Grillon Silencieux-El Grillo Silencioso
○ Toy 2: The Grouchy Ladybug-La Petite Coccinelle Qui Voulait se Battre-La Mariquita Malhumorada
○ Toy 3: The Very Busy Spider-L'Araignee Besogneuse-Una Aran*a Muy Occupada
○ Toy 4: The Very Hungry Caterpillar-La Chinelle Affamee-La Oruga Muy Hambrienta
○ Toy 5: A House for Hermit Crab-Une Maison Pour Bernard L'Ermite-Una Casa Para el Hermitano
○ Toy 6: The Very Busy Bee

McDonald's 1996, $1 each-6 per set & U-3.

Markings. "© 1990 by Eric Carle Corp"

Row 3: Fisher Price Under-3 Toys

○ Toy 1: Birdie   ○ Toy 5: Turning Beads
○ Toy 2: Ronald   ○ Toy 6: Boom Box Rattle
○ Toy 3: Grimace   ○ Toy 7: Dog House
○ Toy 4: Book   ○ Toy 8: Slide Puzzle

McDonald's 1996, $1-2 each. These toys are not related to the regular offerings.

Markings: "© 1996 Fisher-Price Inc Mfg for and distributed by McDonald's ©1996 McDonald's China"

Row 4: Hot Wheels 95

○ Toy 1: Lightning Speed-Eclair Fulgurant-Relampago
○ Toy 2: Shock Force-Puissance Choc-Impulsor
○ Toy 3: Twin Engine-Double Turbo-Bimotor
○ Toy 4: Radar Racer-Ultra Radar-Explorador
○ Toy 5: Blue Bandit-Engin Pirate-Bandido Azul
○ Toy 6: Power Circuit-Turbopropulseur-Supersonico
○ Toy 7: Back Burner-Suprasonique-Quemador
○ Toy 8: After Balast-Bolide Foudroyant-Explosiva
○ Toy 9: U-3 Jouet Pour Moins de 3 Ans-menores de 3 An*os Premio

McDonald's 1995, $1-2 each-8 per set & U-3.

Markings: "Hot Wheels ® © 1995 Mattel Inc"

McDonald's

Row 1: Hot Wheels 96
❍ Toy 1: Flame Series
❍ Toy 2: Roarin' Rod Series
❍ Toy 3: Dark Rider
❍ Toy 4: Hot Hubs Series
❍ Toy 5: Krackle Car Series
❍ Toy 6: U-3 Squeek Toy
McDonald's 1996, $1-2 each-5 per set & U-3.
Markings: "Hot Wheels ® China Chine © 1993 Mattel Inc"
Row 2: Littlest Pet Shop ™
❍ Toy 1: Swan-Cygne-Cisne
❍ Toy 2: Unicorn-Licorne-Unicornio
❍ Toy 3: Dragon
❍ Toy 4: Tiger-Tigre
❍ Toy 5: U-3 Hamster in Exercise Wheel
McDonald's 1996, $1-2 each. A TV cartoon series, 4 per set & U-3.

Markings: "©1996 Tonka Corp China"
Row 3: Spiderman
❍ Dr Octopus
See page 83 for the set information
Row 4: Marvel Super Heroes
❍ Toy 1: Spiderman
❍ Toy 2: Storm-Tornade-Tormenta
❍ Toy 3: Wolverine-Serval-Lobezna
❍ Toy 4: Jubilee-Jubile-Jubilo
❍ Toy 5: Color Change Invisible Woman-L'Invisible Cameleon-La Mujer Invisible que Cambia de Color
❍ Toy 6: Thing-La Chose-La Cosa
❍ Toy 7: Hulk- La Masa
❍ Toy 8: Human Torch-La Torche-La Antorcha Humana
❍ Toy 9: U-3 Spiderman Ball
McDonald's 1996, $1-2 each-8 per set & U-3.
Markings: "©1996 Marvel China"

McDonald's

Row 1: McDonald's Halloween McCharacters
- ○ Toy 1: Frankenstein Ronald
- ○ Toy 2: Pumpkin Birdie
- ○ Toy 3: Bat-Burglar
- ○ Toy 4: Ghost Grimace
- ○ Toy 5: U-3 Grimace

McDonald's 1995, $1-3 each-3 pieces each, 4 per set & U-3.
Markings: "McDonald's China"

Row 2: McNugget Buddies Halloween
- ○ Toy 1: Clown
- ○ Toy 2: Monster
- ○ Toy 3: Princess
- ○ Toy 4: Dragon
- ○ Toy 5: Rock Star
- ○ Toy 6: Octopus

McDonald's 1996, $2-3 each-3 pieces each, 6 per set.
Markings: "©1995 McDonald's Corp China"

NO markings on costume pieces.

Row 3: Muppet Treasure Island
- ○ Toy 1: Miss Piggy
- ○ Toy 2: Kermit-2 pieces
- ○ Toy 3: Fozzie
- ○ Toy 4: Gonzo
- ○ Toy 5: U-3 Book for Bath

McDonald's 1996, $1-2 each. A motion picture, 4 per set & U-3.
Markings: "©1995 Henson China"

Row 4: Power Rangers
- ○ Toy 1: Power Siren
- ○ Toy 2: Power Com
- ○ Toy 3: Powermorpher ™ Buckle-4 pieces
- ○ Toy 4: Alien Detector
- ○ Toy 5: U-3 Power Flute

McDonald's 1995, $1-3 each. A TV series, 4 per set & U-3.
Markings: "™ & © 1995 TCFFC ™ & © 1995 Saban China"

McDonald's

McDonald's

Row 1: Snow White
○ Sleepy
See page 81 for the set information

Row 2: Richard Scarry
○ Toy 1: Lowly Worm & Post Office-Asticot et Bureau de Poste-Gusy y Correo
○ Toy 2: Huckle Cat & School-Cassis et Ecole-Felipe y Escuela
○ Toy 3: Mr Frumble & Fire Station-Monsieur Maladroit et Caserne de Pompiers-Sr Lioso y Los Bomberos
○ Toy 4: Bananas Gorilla & Grocery Store-Peau de Banane et Epicerie-Gorilla Banana y Tienda de Comestibles
○ Toy 5: U-3 Lowly Worm-Asticot-Gusy
McDonald's 1995, $1-2 each-3 pieces each, 4 per set & U-3.
Markings: ©94 ® Richard Scarry China Chine"

Row 3: Space Jam
○ Toy 1: Lola Bunny
○ Toy 2: Bugs Bunny
○ Toy 3: Marvin the Martian
○ Toy 4: Daffy
○ Toy 5: Taz
○ Toy 6: Monstar
○ Toy 7: Sylvester & Tweety
○ Toy 8: Nerdlucks
McDonalds 1996, $2-4 each. A motion picture, all link together and move, 8 per set. *Markings:* "™ & © 1996 Warner Bros"

Row 4: Tangle
○ 8 Toys
McDonald's 1997, $1 each. All link together, 2 pieces each.
Markings: "© 1996 Mattel Inc"

Row 1: Totally Toy Holiday 95

○ Toy 1: Holiday Barbie Figurine-Figurine Barbie Joyeuses Getes-Figura Barbie Gran Gala

○ Toy 2: Hot Wheels Vehicle with Ramp-Vehicule et Rampe-Vehiculo y Ramo

○ Toy 3: Polly Pocket ™ Playset-Coffret-Estuche

○ Toy 4: Mighty Max Playset-Coffret-Estuche

○ Toy 5: Cabbage Patch ™ Playset-Coffret-Estuche

○ Toy 6: Hot Wheels ™ North Pole Explorer-Explorateur du Pole Nord-Explorador del Polonorte

Row 2:

○ Toy 7: "Once Upon a Dream ™ Princess Figurine- "Il Etait une Fois" Une Princesse-"Princesa de Tus Suen*os"

○ Toy 8: "Great Adventures" Knight Figurine-Figurine de Chevalier-Figura Caballero Grandes Aventuras-2 pieces

○ Toy 9: U-3 Key Car

○ Toy 10: U-3 Baby Girl

Row 3: Transformers

○ Toy 1: Manta Ray-Raie Mante-Manta Raya

○ Toy 2: Beetle-Coleoptera-Escarabajo

○ Toy 3: Panther-Panthere-Pantera

○ Toy 4: Rhino-Rhinaceros-Rinocerante

○ Toy 5: U-3 Lion/Robot

McDonald's 1996, $1-2 each

Markings: "© 1996 Hasbro © 1996 Takera Chine"

Row 4: VR Troopers

○ Toy 1: Kaleidoscope

○ Toy 2: Wrist Spinner-3 pieces

○ Toy 3: Crystal Necklace

○ Toy 4: Visor

○ Toy 5: U-3 Sphere

McDonald's 1996, $2-4 each

Markings: "™ & © 1995 Saban China"

McDonald's

Row 1: Walt Disney Masterpiece Collection
❍ Toy 1: Cinderella
❍ Toy 2: Alice in Wonderland-2 pieces
❍ Toy 3: Pocahontas
❍ Toy 4: Snow White
Row 2:
❍ Toy 1: Aristocats
❍ Toy 2: Robin Hood
❍ Toy 3: Aladdin
❍ Toy 4: Sword in the Stone
❍ Toy 5: U-3 Dumbo
McDonald's 1996, $1-2 each. Came in Video-Like Boxes, 8 per set & U-3.
Markings: "© Disney China"

Nathan's

Franksters 95
❍ Superdog
Nathan's Famous Hot Dogs 1995, $5-10 each-4-5 (?) per set.
Markings: "Since 1916 Nathan's ® © (logo) 1995 Nathan's Famous Inc Made in China"

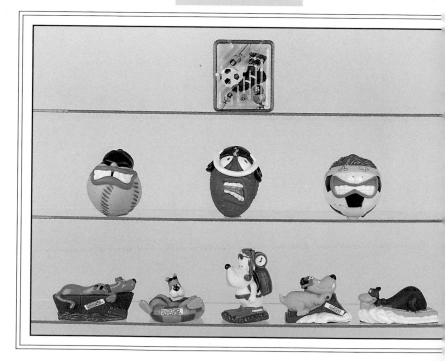

Showbiz Pizza

Row 1: Chuck E Cheese Prizes
○ Toy 1: Transparent Chuck E Cheese
○ Toy 2: Trailer
Showbiz Pizza 1994, $1-3 each
Markings: "© 1992 Showbiz Pizza Time Inc"
Row 2: Showbiz Theater Band
○ Toy 1: Billy Bob
○ Toy 2: Fatz
Showbiz Pizza 1986, $5-6 each
Markings: "©1986 Showbiz Pizza Time Inc Made in China"

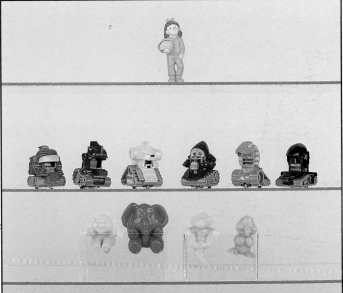

Pizza Hut

Pizza Head A-maze-ing Mazes
○ Super Soccer
Also: Gotta Run!, Trail Blazers, & Hooked on Fishing
Pizza Hut 1996, $2-4 each-4 per set.
Markings: "© 1996 Pizza Hut Inc, Made in China"
Row 2: Sports Balls
○ Toy 1: Baseball
○ Toy 2: Football
○ Toy 3: Soccer Ball
Pizza Hut 1994, $2-3 each-3 per set.
Markings: "© Pizza Hut Inc 1994 Made in China"
Row 3: Squirt Toons
○ Toy 1: Scooby Doo
○ Toy 2: Astro
○ Toy 3: Droopy
○ Toy 4: Muttley
○ Toy 5: Dino
Pizza Hut 1996, $1-3 each. Water squirters, 5 per set.
Markings: "©1995 TEC Made in China" Printed logo: "Cartoon Network ®"

Sonic

Adventures of the Super Sonic Kids
○ Corkey
See page 92 for the set information
Row 2: Cy-Treds
○ Toy 1: Beek
○ Toy 2: Flame
○ Toy 3: Jab
○ Toy 4: Bolt
○ Toy 5: Coil
○ Toy 6: Skull
Sonic Drive-Ins 1996, $2-4
each. Also given out by McDonald's and Subway, 6 per set.
Markings: "Sonic RG*Made in China"
Row 3: Fluorescent Glass Hangers
○ Toy 1: Cat
○ Toy 2: Elephant
○ Toy 3: Alligator
○ Toy 4: Bird
Sonic Drive-Ins 1997, $1-2 each-9 per set.
No markings.

Sonic

Sonic

Row 1: Food Racers
○ Ice Cream Soda
Also: others
Sonic Drive-Ins 1996, $1-3 each.
Printed: "© 1996 Sonic Made in China"
Row 2: Food Train
○ Toy 1: Sonic Chili Flat
○ Toy 2: Sonic Mustard
Also: Sonic Engine and Sonic Caboose
Sonic Drive-Ins 1996, $2-4 each-4 per set. Printed: "© 1995 Sonic Made in China"
Row 3: Planet Balls
○ Jupiter
Also: Moon, Mars, Earth, Saturn, and Neptune
Sonic Drive-Ins 1994, $2-4 each.
Also given out by Denny's, 6 per set. Printed: "Sonic America's Drive In ® (logo)"
Row 4: World Turtle
○ World Turtle
Sonic Drive-Ins 1996, $2-3 each.
Printed: "©1996 Sonic China"

Subway

Row 1: All Dogs Go To
Heaven 2

○ Toy 1: Charlie   ○ Toy 4: Sasha
○ Toy 2: Itchy   ○ Toy 5: Carface
○ Toy 3: David

Subway 1996, $2-4 each. A cartoon motion
picture, All Dogs Go To Heaven I characters were
given by Wendy's, 5 per set.
Markings: "™ & © 1996 MGM ™ Subway (logo) ©
96 JGI & DAI China"

Row 2: Beekman's World

○ Toy 1: Color Changing Penguins Don and Herb
○ Toy 2: Flip Top
Also: 2 others
Subway 1995, $2-3 each-4 per set.
Markings: "Beekman's World (logo) subway ®
(logo) ©1995 Elp Communications © JGI & DAI
China"

Row 3: Bobby's World

○ Toy 1: Bobby   ○ Toy 3: Knight
○ Toy 2: Astronaut   ○ Toy 4: Cowboy
Subway 1995, $2-4 each. A TV cartoon series, 4
per set.
Markings: "© PCN 1995 Mfg for Subway (logo) by
JGI"

Row 4: Bump in the Night

○ Toy 1: Destructo ™   ○ Toy 3: Mr Bump ™
○ Toy 2: Molly ™   ○ Toy 4: Squishington ™
Subway 1995, $3-4 each. A TV cartoon series, 4
per set.
Markings: "Subway (logo) by JGI China"

Subway

Row 1: Coral Reefs

○ Toy 1: U-3 Pink Fish   ○ Toy 3: U-3 Green Fish
○ Toy 2: U-3 Yellow Fish
Subway 1995, $2-3 each. The regular offering was inflatable fish,
4 per set and 3 U-3's
No markings.

Row 2: Dinosaurs

○ Toy 1: Baby-4 pieces   ○ Toy 4: Earl
○ Toy 2: Robbie   ○ Toy 5: Fran
○ Toy 3: Charlene
Subway 1996, $2-4 each. A TV series, each character has a jigsaw
puzzle piece as a stand, 5 per set.
Markings: "Subway ® (logo) Disney ©1995 JGI & DAI China"

Row 3: Speedsters

○ Toy 1: Rocket Racer   ○ Toy 3: Red Racer
○ Toy 2: Radical Roadster   ○ Toy 4: Star Spangled
Speedster
Subway 1996, $2-5 each. Each came with 3 road signs, 4 per set,
4 pieces each.
Markings: "Subway ® (logo) ©1996 JGI & DAI"
No markings on signs

Row 4: Spiderman

○ Toy 1: Spider Rider   ○ Toy 2: Spider Glider
Also: 3 others
Subway 1996, $4-5 each-5 per set.
Markings: "Subway ® (logo) ©1996 JGI & DAI ™ & ©1996 Marvel
China"

173

Taco Bell

Row 1: Ace Ventura

○ Toy 1: For The Birds Feeder-2 pieces
○ Toy 2: Rainforest Runaway-car launcher-3 pieces
○ Toy 3: Unpredictaball
○ Toy 4: Nesting Pets-2 pieces
Taco Bell 1996, $1-2 each-4 per set.
Markings: "MFG by Strottman Intl Inc China ™ & © 1996 Morgan Creek Productions Inc"

Row 2: Desert Cruisers

○ Toy 1: Packrabbit on Slug-Red Car
○ Toy 2: Slobo on Fish-Blue Car
○ Toy 3: Mo on Road-Pink Caddy
○ Toy 4: El Sid on Tarantula-Purple Car
Taco Bell 1996, $1-3 each
Markings: "© 1995 UCS ™ Shiny Strottman Int'l Inc Made in China"

Row 3: Earthworm Jim

○ Toy 1: Worm Launcher-pops head out
○ Toy 2: Bowlin' with Bob
○ Toy 3: Rocket Ripper-Rev-Up
○ Toy 4: Peter Puppy and Monster Dog
Taco Bell 1996, $1-2 each-4 per set.
Markings: "© 1995 UCS ™ Shiny Strottman Int'l Inc Made in China"

Row 4: Flintstones' Stone Age Stampers

○ Toy 1: Dino-"Dino surfing on alligator" picture-roller stamper
○ Toy 2: Barney-"Barney on motorcycle" picture
○ Toy 3: Pebbles-"Pebbles in carriage" picture
○ Toy 4: Fred-"Fred playing golf picture"-roller stamper
Taco Bell 1995 $1-3 each. Stampers, a TV cartoon series, 4 per set
Markings: "©1995 HBPI Made in China"

Taco Bell

Row 1: Goosebumps
○ Toy 1: Slappy's Candy Keeper
○ Toy 2: Cuddles the Horrible Hamster
○ Toy 3: Skullmobile
○ Toy 4: Wrappin' Mummy
Taco Bell 1996, $1-3 each. A TV cartoon series, 4 per set.
Markings: "™ & © Parachute Press Inc Mfg by Strottman Inc China"
Row 2: Kazaam
○ Toy 1: Reach for Riches Water Catch Game
○ Toy 2: Kazaam Street Racer
○ Toy 3: Fortune Finder
○ Toy 4: Boombox Jam Spinner
Taco Bell 1996, $2-4 each. A motion picture, 4 per set.

Markings: "Kazaam ™ © Disney/Interscope Strottman Int'l Inc
Made in China"
Row 3: Life With Louie
○ Spinner
Also: Magic Sketch, Louie's Burstin' Bubble, & Louie's Travel Pak
Taco Bell 1996, $1-2 each-4 per set.
Markings: "By Strottman Int'l Inc China"
Row 4: Masked Rider
○ Toy 1: Secret Hideaway Belt Clip with Figurine-2 pieces
○ Toy 2: Sword Mystery-8 pieces
○ Toy 3: Mystic Chamber-3 pieces
○ Toy 4: Transforming Vehicles-3 pieces
Taco Bell 1996, $2-3 each-4 per set.
Markings: "™ & © 1996 Saban Made in
China Applause"

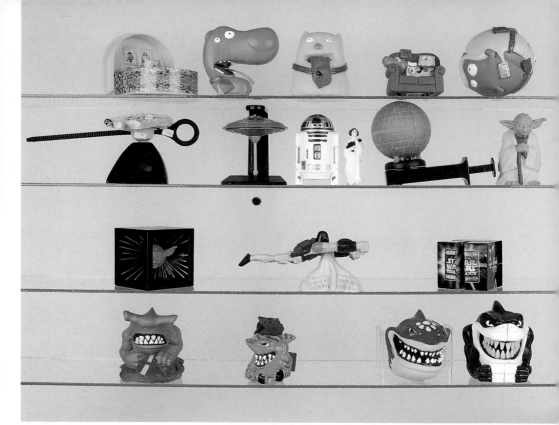

Taco Bell

Row 1: Nacho and Dog
- Toy 1: Nacho and Dog Taco House-2 pieces
- Toy 2: Dog Pick-A-Sticker
- Toy 3: Nacho Rad Razzzer
- Toy 4: Nacho and Dog Couch Mobile
- Toy 5: U-3 Nacho and Dog Ball

Taco Bell 1996, $1-4 each-4 per set & U-3.
Markings: "Nacho and Dog ™ © 1995 Taco Bell Crop Strottman Int'l Inc Made in China"

Row 2: Star Wars
- Toy 1: Millennium Falcon Gyro-3 pieces
- Toy 2: Floating Cloud City-2 pieces
- Toy 3: R-2 D-2 Playset with Princess Leia-2 pieces
- Toy 4: Exploding Death Star Spinner
- Toy 5: U-3 Yoda

Row 3:
- Toy 6: Magic Cube
- Toy 7: Balancing Boba Fett-2 pieces
- Toy 8: Puzzle Cube

Also: Magic Cube, Balancing Boba Fett, & Puzzle Cube
Taco Bell 1997, $3-5 each. A motion picture series, The Death Star Spinner was recalled and reissued with more "sparkle", 7 per set & U-3.
Markings: "© 1996 Lucasfilm Ltd Applause China"

Row 4: Street Sharks
- Toy 1: Jab Street Squirter
- Toy 2: Streex Wrist Crunch'r
- Toy 3: Big Shammy Jawsome

Chomper
- Toy 4: Ripster Grusome Toothsome

Taco Bell 1995, $1-2 each. A TV cartoon series, 4 per set.
Markings: "©1995 Street Wise Designs Inc © 1995 Strottman International Inc"

Taco Bell

Row 1: The Mask
- Toy 1: It's Party Time! Light Switch Cover
- Toy 2: Milo with Mask-pencil topper
- Toy 3: Ooze N Form with Wacky Dough-dough & press
- Toy 4: Somebody sssss Top Me!

Taco Bell 1995, $1-2 each. A TV cartoon series, 4 per set.
Markings: "© & ™ 1995 New Line Prod Inc Strottman Int'l Inc Made in China"

Row 2: The Tick
- Toy 1: Thrakkorzog Squirter
- Toy 2: Arthur Wall Climber
- Toy 3: The Tick Power Roller
- Toy 4: U-3 The Tick Finger Puppet

Also: The Tick Superhero Sheets
Taco Bell 1995, $2-4 each. A TV cartoon series, 4 per set & U-3.
Markings: "© FCN China"

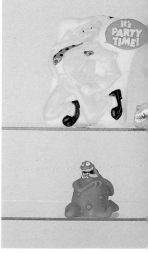

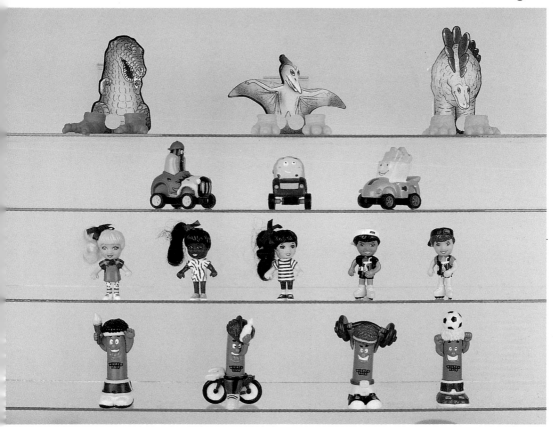

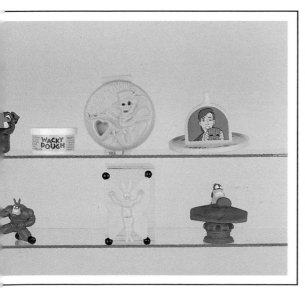

Target

Row 1: Dino Tracks
○ Toy 1: Tyranosaurus Rex
○ Toy 2: Pteradactyl
○ Toy 3: Stegosaurus
Target Stores 1995, $1-2 each. Paper finger puppets with rubber feet for the finger tips, 3 per set.
Markings: "® Food Avenue 1994" or "Target Stores ®"
Row 2: Target Food on Wheels
○ Toy 1. "Hot Dogger"
○ Toy 2: "Cheesy"
○ Toy 3: "March-5 Fries"
Also: Hamburger
Target Stores 1996, $1-3 each-4 per set.
Markings: "China"
Row 3: Targeteers
○ Toy 1: Ashley
○ Toy 2: Danielle
○ Toy 3: Mei-Ling
○ Toy 4: Ramon
○ Toy 5: Buddy
Target Stores 1993, $4-5 each-5 per set
Markings: "Made in China"
Row 4: Weiner Pack Olympic Sports Figures
○ Toy 1: Torch Runner
○ Toy 2: Cycle Racer
○ Toy 3: Weight Lifter
○ Toy 4: Soccer Player
Target Stores 1996, $2-4 each. 3 pieces each, 4 per set.
Markings: "Food Avenue Target Stores ® Hillshire Farms © 1996 Made in China"

Wendy's

Row 1: Animalinks
- Toy 1: Monkey
- Toy 2: Dog
- Toy 3: Alligator
- Toy 4: Giraffe
- Toy 5: Octopus
- Toy 6: U-3 About Face-stacking blocks

Wendy's 1995, $1-2 each. Novelty ink pens, 2 pieces each, U-3 3 pieces, 5 per set & U-3
Markings: "©1995 Wendy's Int'l Inc China"

Row 2: Ball Players
- Toy 1: Football
- Toy 2: Baseball
- Toy 3: Basketball
- Toy 4: Tennis Ball
- Toy 5: U-3 Kickball

Wendy's 1995, $1-3 each-4 per set & U-3.
Markings: "© 1995 Wendy's Int'l Inc China"

Row 3: Bike Trax
- Toy 1: Riding
- Toy 2: Spoke Reflector
- Toy 3: Spoke Reflector

Also: other bike gear-a horn and pouch and water bottle

Wendy's 1995, $2-4 each
Markings: "©1995 Wendy's Int'l Inc China"

Row 4: Cartoons
- Toy 1: Hot Rod
- Toy 2: U-3 Stretch Limo
- Toy 3: Convertible
- Toy 4: Police Car
- Toy 5: Split-Apart Molasses Truck

Wendy's 1996, $1-2 each-4 per set & U-3.
Markings: "©1996 Wendy's Int'l Inc China"

Wendy's

Row 1: Club Cave
- Toy 1: Pick Up Bones-24 bones
- Toy 2: Dino Skeleton-9 pieces & egg
- Toy 3: Dino Bank
- Toy 4: Wrist Watch

Wendy's 1997, $1-2 each-4 per set.
Markings: "Club Cave © 1996 Wendy's Int'l Inc China"

Row 2: Felix The Cat 96
- Toy 1: Zoetrope
- Toy 2: Milk Caps
- Toy 3: Plush
- Toy 4: Psychic
- Toy 5: U-3 Rub on Set of 3

Also: Story Board
Wendy's 1996, $2-3 each-5 per set & U-3.
Markings: "™ Felix The Cat Productions Inc © Made in China"

Row 3: Felix The Cat 97
- Toy 1: Trophy Winner
- Toy 2: Plush
- Toy 3: Catch Game

Also: 3-D Picture & Shoelaces
Wendy's 1997, $1-3 each-5 per set
Markings: "™ Felix The Cat Productions Inc Made in China"

Wendy's

Row 1: GoBot
- Breez-Helicopter

See page 108 for the set information

Row 2: Laser Knights
- Toy 1: Dragon Warrior
- Toy 2: Charging Armored Knight
- Toy 3: U-3 Roman Centurian-2 pieces
- Toy 4: Winged Warrior
- Toy 5: Knight Warrior

Wendy's 1996, $1-3 each-4 per set & U-3.

Markings: "© Wendy's Int'l Inc China"

Row 3: Mega Wheels
- Toy 1: "2D-Beach!" Beach Buggy
- Toy 2: "Groovin!" Flower Power

- Toy 3: "Yeeha!" Western Pick Up
- Toy 4: "Vroom!" Hot Rod
- Toy 5: "N2 Tunes" Rock & Roller
- Toy 6: U-3 Circus Wagon-no stickers

Wendy's 1996, $1-2 each. Stickers for details, 5 per set & U-3.

Markings: "© 1995 Wendy's Int'l Inc"

Row 4: Robot Games
- Toy 1: Spiral Game
- Toy 2: Robot Shoot
- Toy 3: Spaceship Maze
- Toy 4: Maze with Spinning Robot Head-2 pieces
- Toy 5: U-3 Domino Match Game-cards

Wendy's 1996, $1-2 each-4 per set & U-3.

Markings: "©1996 Wendy's Int'l Dublin Ohio"

Wendy's
Row 1: Surprise!
❍ Toy 1: Driving Dino
❍ Toy 2: Frog Squirter
❍ Toy 3: Dino Mouth
❍ Toy 4: Clam Viewer
❍ Toy 5: Turtle
❍ Toy 6: U-3 Dino Egg
Also: pogs, cards, & stickers
Wendy's 1995, $1-3 each.
Various toys in 3 eggs of 3
colors each, 9 per set &
U-3. *Markings:* "©1995
Wendy's Int'l Inc"
Row 2: Saurus Sports Balls
❍ Soccerasaurus
See page 111 for the set
information
Row 3: Way 2 Go!
❍ Toy 1: Tire Water Bottle
❍ Toy 2: Travel Match
Game
❍ Toy 3: U-3 Identification
Bracelet
Also: postcards & another game
Wendy's 1996, $1-2 each-4 per set & U-3.
Markings: "©1996 Wendy's Int'l Inc China"

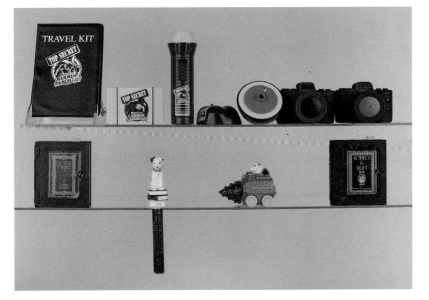

Wendy's
Row 1: Where is Carmen Sandiego?
❍ Toy 1: Travel Kit
❍ Toy 2: Gum Pack/Compass
❍ Toy 3: Flashlight/Spyglass
❍ Toy 4: Apple Decoder-2 pieces
❍ Toy 5 & 6: U-3 Squirt Cameras
Also: Magazine
Wendy's 1996, $1-3 each-6 per set & U-3.
Markings: "® Broderbund Software Inc Wendy's

Int'l Inc China"
Row 2: Wishbone
❍ Toy 1: "Oliver Twist" Book Viewer
❍ Toy 2: Wishbone Pen-2 pieces
❍ Toy 3: Wishbone Earth Digger
❍ Toy 4: "Romeo & Juliet" Book Viewer
Also: Booklet & Stickers
Wendy's 1996, $1-3 each-5 per set.
Markings: "© 1996 Wendy's Int'l Inc China"

FOREIGN

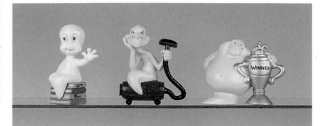

Casper
○ Toy 1: Casper on Books
○ Toy 2: Stinkie on Ghost Vac
○ Toy 3: Fatso with Winner Trophy
Also: Stretch
Quick 1994, $10 each. A motion picture, 4 per set.
Markings: "Casper © 1994 UCS & Amblin ™ Harvey Tyco Playtime Inc Made in China" Printed: "Q Quick (logo in red)"

Disneyland Paris
○ Toy 1: Mickey in Castle
○ Toy 2: Minnie in Cottage
○ Toy 3: Daisy in Tent

○ Toy 4: Donald in Silo
McDonald's Europe 1996, $5-10. Buildings open up and characters pop up and

spread arms, 4 per set.
Markings: "Disneyland Paris ® © Disney China"
Row 1: McFood Races

McFood Races
○ Toy 1: Big Mac
○ Toy 2: Shake
○ Toy 3: Fries
○ Toy 4: Hamburger
McDonald's Europe 1993, $5-10 each. Wind-up food that roll around on tracks peel-off stickers, 4 per set, 2 pieces each.
Markings: "© 1993 McDonald's Corp China" 2 are marked: "1995"
Row 2: McFarm
○ Toy 1: Farmer Ronald
○ Toy 2: Grimace Harvesting Corn
○ Toy 3: Birdie Pushing Chicken Nest
○ Toy 4: Hamburglar Bailing Hay
McDonald's Europe 1995, $5-10 each-4 per set.

Markings: "© 1995 McDonald's Corp China"
Row 3: McRodeo
○ Toy 1: Bullseye Ronald-pop up

○ Toy 2: Birdie-spins lasso
○ Toy 3: Grimace on Bronco
○ Toy 4: Partner Hamburglar-rotates head

McDonald's Europe 1995, $5-10 each-4 per set.
Markings: "© 1995 MCD Corp China"

Tom & Jerry Catch The Excitement
O Toy 1: Tom on Skateboard Racer
O Toy 2: Jerry on Cheese Racer
O Toy 3: Tom Finger Puppet in Race Car-2 pieces
O Toy 4: Jerry Finger Puppet in Race Car-2 pieces
Burger King Europe 1995, $7-10 each-4 per set.
Markings: "© 1995 Turner Entertainment Co"

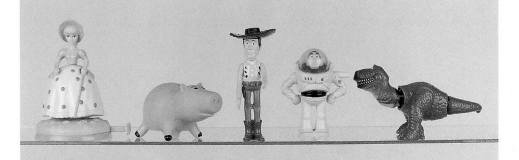

Toy Story
O Toy 1: Bo-Peep-spinner
O Toy 2: Hamm-bank
O Toy 3: Woody-arms move
O Toy 4: Buzz Lightyear-wind-up walker
O Toy 5: Rex-bobs
McDonald's 1996, $5-10 each. A Disney cartoon motion picture, 5 per set.
Markings: "Disney © China"

PLUSH & BIG
A & W Bear Sipper
O Toy 1: A & W Sipper
O Toy 2: A & W Plush Bear
A & W Drive-Ins 1994, $1-12. About 9"sipper, plush is about 3-3/4" which is the smallest of several sizes that were sold in the restaurants.
Markings: "©1994 A & W Restaurants Inc Made in Canada"

Left:
Air Garfield
○ Inflatable
Pizza Hut 1993, $2-4
each. About 8"
diameter
No markings.

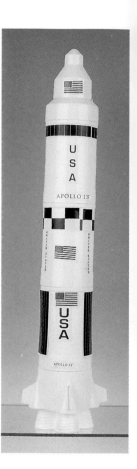

Right:
Apollo 13
○ Toy 1: Nose Cone
○ Toy 2: Mid Section
○ Toy 3: Booster Rockets
Hardee's 1995, $5-8. A motion picture,
each section came with a screw off lid,
giving 2 extra containers, each with Pogs
and peel-off stickers, about 15" long.
Markings: "AGC Pat Pending"

Babe
Row 1: Babe
○ Toy 1: Babe
○ Toy 2: Cow-La Vache-La Vaca
○ Toy 3: Maa
○ Toy 4: Fly-Fecelle-Flecha
Row 2:
○ Toy 5: Ferdinand-Fernando
○ Toy 6: Duchess-Duchesse-Duquesa
○ Toy 7: Mouse-La Souris-El Raton
McDonald's 1996, $1 each. A motion picture, about 3" tall, 7 per set. Tag: "© 1995
McDonald's Corp"

Burger King Kids Sippers
- Toy 1: IQ
- Toy 2: Snaps
- Toy 3: Jaws
- Toy 4: Kid Vid
- Toy 5: Boomer

Burger King 1996, $1-2 each. About 9" tall, 5 per set 4 pieces each.
Markings: "Burger King Kid's Club (logo) © 1995 Burger King Corp"

Chester Cheeta
- Fast Flyin' Disc

Also: Spotted Summer Shades, Mini Wrist-Pack, Totally Fun Visor, & Inflatable Bobble Ball
Kentucky Fried Chicken 1996, $1-3 each. About 7" diameter, 5 per set.
Markings: "Chester Cheeta®"

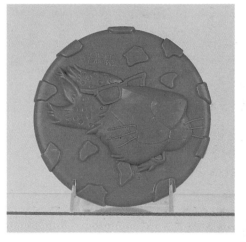

Chuck E Cheese
- Toy 1: 9" disc
- Toy 2: Halloween Sipper
- Toy 3: Bendable Chuck E Cheese
- Toy 4: Chuck E Cheese in Tux Bank

Showbiz Pizza 1991, $2-6 each
Markings: "© Showbiz Pizza Time Inc 1992 Produced by Dennis Eoland Inc"

Coca Cola

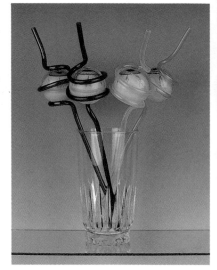

Coca Cola Bear
❍ Coca Cola Polar Bear
Long John Silvers 1995, $7-10. About 9 1/2" sitting. Tag: "Coca Cola ® Brand Plush Collection"

Eyes
❍ Toy 1: Creature Eye
❍ Toy 2: Frankenstein Eye
❍ Toy 3: Mad Scientist Eye
❍ Toy 4: Hypno Eye
Taco Bell 1996, $2-4 each. Water balls 2" diameter, 12" straws.
No markings

Dippers
❍ Toy 1: Whale
❍ Toy 2: Clam
Dairy Queen 1996, $1-2 each. About 10" long.
Markings: "China"

Flipper
❍ Toy 1: Flipper
❍ Toy 2: Scar
Pizza Hut 1996, $3-5 each.
Squirting hand puppets, about 7" high, 2 per set.
Markings: "Flipper (logo) ™ CR TFG Made in China"

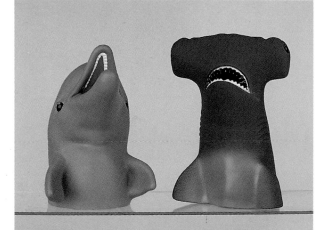

Hunchback of Notre Dame Hand Puppets
○ Toy 1: Hugo
○ Toy 2: Phoebus
○ Toy 3: Esmeralda
○ Toy 4: Quasimodo
Burger King 1996, $2-4 each. About 9" tall, a Disney cartoon motion picture, 4 per set. Tag: "Mfg for Burger King Corp © Disney"

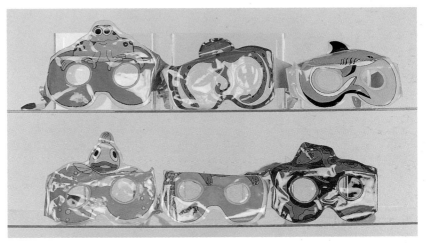

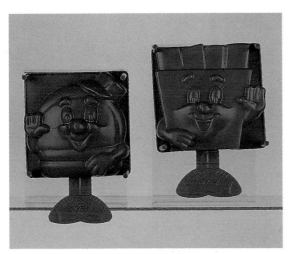

Inflatable Water Goggles
Row 1:
○ Toy 1: Frog   ○ Toy 3: Shark
○ Toy 2: Octopus
Row 2:
○ Toy 4: Fish   ○ Toy 6: Snake
○ Toy 5: Alligator
Long John Silvers 1996, $1-3 each. About 4" high, 6 per set.
No markings.

Krystal Freezer Treats
○ Toy 1: Miss Fries
○ Toy 2: Krystal
Also: Corn Pup & Drink
Krystal 1996, $1-2 each. Freezer tray shaped like 4 Krystal Kids, about 4" high, 4 per set.
Markings: "Krystal ® (logo)"

Krystal Freezer Treats

Row 1: Krystal Kids Flyers
- Toy 1: Drink
- Toy 2: Miss Fries
- Toy 3: Corn Pup

Row 2:
- Toy 4: Krystal
- Toy 5: Hot Dog

Krystal 1995, $2-3 each. About 7" diameter, 5 per set.
Printed: "© 1995 The Krystal Company"

Muppet Puppet Football Cups
- Toy 1: Gonzo
- Toy 2: Miss Piggy
- Toy 3: Kermit
- Toy 4: Fozzie

Dairy Queen 1996, $2-4 each. Muppets are finger puppets on lids, 3 pieces each, 4 per set.
Markings: "© Henson CDM "

Papa John's Flyer
- Papa John's Flyer

Papa John's Pizza 1995, $2-5. About 9" diameter.
Markings: "Enduro USA"

Power Rangers
Row 1: Power Rangers the Movie
○ Toy 1: Black Ranger with Frog Ninjazord
○ Toy 2: Yellow Ranger with Bear Ninjazord
○ Toy 3: Red Ranger with Ape Ninjazord
Row 2:
○ Toy 4: White Ranger with Falcon Ninjazord
○ Toy 5: Pink Ranger with Crane Ninjazord
○ Toy 6: Blue Ranger with Wolf Ninjazord
McDonald's 1995, $2-4 each. A motion picture,
figurines about 4" tall, 6 per set.
Markings: "™ & ©1995 TCFFC TN* & © 1995
Saban"

Rocketeer
○ Rocketeer Sipper
Pizza Hut 1991, $1-2. A motion
picture, about 7" tall, 2 pieces.
Markings: "Miner"

Shark!
Row 1:
○ Toy 1: U-3 Sand Toys-also in red
○ Toy 2: Water Bottle
○ Toy 3: Shark Squirter
Row 2:
○ Toy 4: Shark Wallet
○ Toy 5: Inflatable Shark
○ Toy 6: Inflatable Shark Viewer Boat
Wendy's 1996, $1-2 each. About 6" tall, 5 per set & U-3.
Markings: "Wendy's Int'l Inc China"

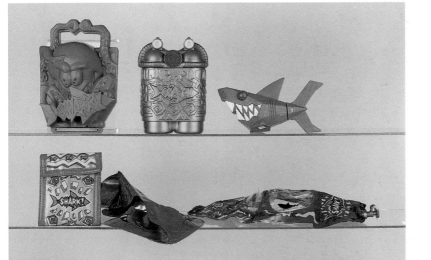

Shoney Bear Bank
○ Bank
Shoney Restaurants
1993, $4-6. About 8"
tall.
Markings: "Shoney Bear
is s Registered
Trademark ® of
Shoneys Inc"

Space Jam

Space Jam

Row 1: Space Jam
- ○ Toy 1: Nerdluck
- ○ Toy 2: Monstars Blanko
- ○ Toy 3: Nerdluck
- ○ Toy 4: Daffy

Row 2:
- ○ Toy 5: Bugs Bunny
- ○ Toy 6: Lola Bunny
- ○ Toy 7: Taz

McDonald's 1996, $2-3 each. A motion picture from 4"-10", both Nerdlucks came packaged together, 6 per set. Tag: "Warner Brothers (logo) © 1996 Warner Bros © 1996 McDonald's Corporation"

The Tick

Row 1: The Tick
- ○ Toy 1: The Tick Balance-2 pieces
- ○ Toy 2: Arthur Soars-3 pieces

Row 2:
- ○ Toy 3: Charles The Brain Child-catch game
- ○ Toy 4: Sewer Urchin-3 pieces

Taco Bell 1996, $1-3 each. From 4"-8"
Markings: "©1996 FCN Applause PWI Made in China"

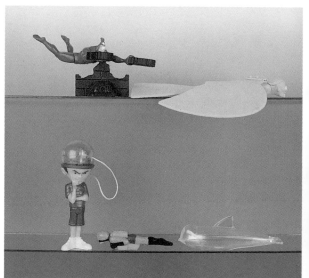

Toy Story
Row 1: Toy Story
❍ Toy 1: Talking Woody
❍ Toy 2: Race Car-3 pieces
Row 2:
❍ Toy 3: Buzz Lightyear
Burger King 1996, $2-3 each. From
7"-10", 3 per set.
Markings: "Mfg for Burger King Corp
© Disney China"

Toy Story
Row 1: Toy Story Hand Puppets
❍ Toy 1: Woody
❍ Toy 2: Hamm
Row 2:
❍ Toy 3: Buzz Lightyear
❍ Toy 4: Rex
Burger King 1996, $1-3 each. A Disney
cartoon motion picture, about 7"-10, 4 per
set. Tag: "Manufactured for Burger King
Corporation © Disney ©Pixar Made in
China"

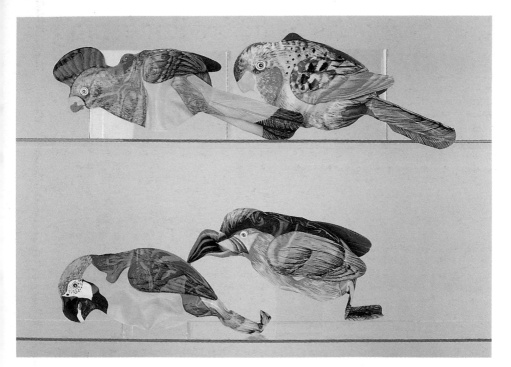

Tropical Birds

Row 1: Tropical Birds
- ○ Toy 1: Great Blue Turaco
- ○ Toy 2: Crimson Rosella

Row 2:
- ○ Toy 3: Blue & Yellow Macaw
- ○ Toy 4: Plate Billed Mountain Toucan

Subway 1996 $1-2 each Inflatables, up to 12" long.
No markings.

Yogi & Friends

Row 1: Yogi & Friends Flyers
- ○ Toy 1: Yogi
- ○ Toy 2: Boo-Boo

Row 2:
- ○ Toy 3: Huckleberry Hound
- ○ Toy 4: Quick Draw McGraw

Arby's 1995, $1-2 each. About 6" diameter, lids for buckets, 4 per set.
Markings: "©1995 Arby's Inc ©1995 Hanna Barbera Productions Inc"